Reinvent Yourself

Gerald Ratner
with Rob Moore

www.reinventyourselfbook.co.uk
www.geraldratner.co.uk
www.robmoore.com

Connect with the authors

Gerald Ratner: Facebook: facebook.com/gerald.ratner.3

Twitter: twitter.com/geraldratner

Instagram: instagram.com/ratnergerald

LinkedIn: linkedin.com/in/geraldratner

Rob Moore: Facebook: facebook.com/robmooreprogressive

Twitter: twitter.com/robprogressive

Instagram: instagram.com/robmooreprogressive

LinkedIn: linkedin.com/in/robmoore1979

Published by

Progressive Media
Progressive House, Units 8, 9, & 10
Cygnet Park, Folder Way, Hampton
Peterborough, PE7 8GX

Contents

FOREWORD FROM ROB:
You're about to learn from the poster boy of reinvention

What an extraordinary world we live in. In 2020, the COVID-19 pandemic claimed more than 1 million lives, stopped international travel and put the brakes on the global economy. Businesses dropped like flies, people lost their jobs and there was widespread fear about the future.

Our perspectives changed dramatically in 2020. Things that might have seemed serious early in the year suddenly became insignificant. Remember that Facebook Live no one watched? That meeting you were late for? That one bad review? At the start of 2020, you were probably sweating the small stuff; just a few months later we were facing problems like bailouts, furloughing and death. That's the big stuff.

We faced an emergency on a scale this generation had never witnessed. It's easy to let something like that get on top of you, to give up and wait for it to pass. To ignore what's happening and Netflix and chill. And that might have been all you could manage – the pandemic was a massive trauma, and I don't think suddenly joining the 5am club (which is a load of bollocks anyway, if you ask me) and forcing yourself to hustle (more bollocks) is necessarily the right thing for your mental health in a traumatic situation. We all cope in different ways.

But it wasn't all bad. Some people and companies started really thriving. Amazon was making $10,000 a second and creating thousands of new jobs to fulfil orders. Zoom stocks shot up from just over $70 at the end of January to almost $570 later in the year, going from 10 million to 300 million daily users. Online learning, e-commerce, delivery and remote health services are well suited to a lockdown situation, and they enjoyed the benefits.

On the other side of the coin, some businesses really struggled, and many closed. Airlines were hit hard, with international travel restricted, and global giants like Virgin asked for bailouts. The virus also rang the death knoll for the high street – non-essential stores in the UK closed during lockdown, and the fashion retail industry felt the pressure. Some huge names went into administration – Debenhams, Oasis and Warehouse – and Arcadia Group, which owns Top Shop and Dorothy Perkins, announced that 14,500 of its 16,000 employees were being furloughed.

Others picked up that coin and flipped it themselves. Craft beer company Brewdog temporarily produced hand sanitiser, which it donated to the NHS. Car manufacturers adapted their processes to make ventilators instead of vehicles. Clothing factories shifted to making masks for healthcare workers. And thousands of companies took their products and services online, offering everything from food delivery to yoga lessons (which you might have needed after all the pizza).

I count myself in the coin-flipping group. My property business wasn't seriously affected, but my business partner Mark Homer and I run the UK's biggest property training company, Progressive, and it took a hit. We had to cancel 300 event days at a potential loss of over £6 million in revenue and, unfortunately, we had to furlough more than half of our 95 brilliant employees.

I could have felt sorry for myself, played the victim, stuck my head in the sand and hoped that our cash in the bank would carry the company through this time. Instead, we got our arses in gear and pulled off one of the biggest sales we've ever done – £250,000 in two days in online courses and over £2.5 million in gross sales in the first eight weeks of the lockdown. I count all lockdown money as at least double because of the difficult circumstances, and the situation could easily have resulted in a £1 million loss for us.

I looked at what my clients, fans and followers needed. I ramped up the amount of content I was putting out on social media. I asked people what would help them. And then we made it happen. We launched eight brand new online courses within eight weeks during the lockdown – that's more than we had launched in the previous eight YEARS, and it was because of the lockdown. We focused on e-commerce, online training and how to pivot your business.

We also built a more scalable, remote workforce. I wrote about this in *Life Leverage*: when you get big, you get bloated and you slow down. The lockdown immediately leaned on our decision making, actions and overheads, and forced us to focus ruthlessly on what's most important. Having no choice BUT to survive makes survival far easier and less distracting.

This was the biggest global shift I've ever seen in business. In life. It was new, it was constantly changing, and in many ways, it was terrifying.

But I do think this global shift gave us a huge opportunity. In fact, my word of the pandemic was REINVENTION. I think it represents the biggest opportunity of the decade, even the century. Because the world's biggest problems are the entrepreneur's biggest opportunities.

My co-author: the man behind the biggest corporate blunder of all time

This book has been planned for a long time. Reinvention is a huge topic in business, and as an entrepreneur (especially a disruptive one), I had to stop kicking back against the unknown and embrace change, be flexible, pivot – I had to get used to a continuous process of reinvention. Disrupt or die. Reinvent or face extinction.

I've now written 15 books, and if you follow me already, you'll know that I can talk for hours about any topic you throw at me. The same goes for writing: I've probably got enough content to fill several books about reinvention. But this book needed a different spin – another voice. I wanted the most experienced voice in the world on 'reinvention', and there's no one alive today who has lived reinvention more than this man.

Ever heard the phrase 'doing a Ratner'? I had, and I knew it wasn't positive. It means making a huge blunder in business. But I didn't know the full story until I read Gerald's autobiography, *Gerald Ratner: The Rise and Fall and Rise Again*, in 2006. I absolutely loved it. I loved his down-to-earth nature. I loved his honesty and his dry wit. And his story is amazing, it made me feel like we all have so much to be grateful for. Gerald lost everything, and it was taken from him, I believe, unfairly. Although some people would say he needed bringing back into balance and humility.

As I was reading his book, I thought *one day I'm definitely going to work with Gerald*. I made it happen: Mark and I built our training business, and we hired Gerald to speak. When we met, The Speech was decades behind him. The sting of the shame had worn off and left him with a brilliant story, which he's told on stages around the world. He turned The Speech from a disaster into a success. Isn't it ironic that after making the most disastrous speech ever, he's now making a fortune making a speech about that speech thousands of times, feasting and dining and making an amazing living? That's a great example of how you can turn the very thing that broke your career into your new career. *That* is reinvention. Genius.

So many people had told me he's a fantastic keynote speaker – funny, sharp, self-deprecating – and they were right. He was absolutely brilliant. We've hired him to do lots of speaking gigs since, and he comes with us on our immersive mastermind in the Cayman Islands, where he helps a group of entrepreneurs really flourish. Best of all, he's become a good friend.

To me, his is the ultimate reinvention story. While he buried his head in the sand and hid away for a while, he re-emerged stronger than ever; almost anyone else in his situation would have stayed in bed for the rest of their life. They would have sunk into the devastation and the failure.

They would have taken on the negative picture the press and public were painting. (Even back then, in the early 90s, there were trolls and critics and haters, only they were sharing their negativity on the front pages and the TV screens.)

I think we can learn a lot from other people's stories: we can follow and recreate, build on their successes. But I think it's stories of failure that are even more powerful. Learning about someone else's downfall, their biggest mistakes, their gaffes, their 'Ratners', and finding out how they overcame the failure is so inspiring. It is REAL and not filtered or Photoshopped. And that is exactly how Gerald is.

So when I started to piece together my ideas for this book, I realised that Gerald was the best person on the planet to work on it with. You'll soon come to see why.

A couple of years ago, Gerald and I were in the Cayman Islands doing group mentoring. People were sharing their challenges with the group, and every time someone shared something they were struggling with, Gerald always had the trump card that his challenge had been bigger and more painful than everyone else. He kept us all grounded. It made us feel that our challenges were smaller. That someone else had it worse. That it's ok to struggle. This is part of Gerald's great charm.

The theme kept coming up that if you want to overcome big challenges, the solution is reinvention – reinvent or disrupt an industry, reinvent yourself. If you don't do it to yourself, someone else, your competitor or a global pandemic will. And by then, it could be too late. That theme really manifested its way out while we were doing this group mentoring. In that moment, I realised that I don't think there's anyone on the planet who has had to reinvent themselves more than him. I truly believe the Gerald is the most qualified person living on Earth to talk about reinvention, with his story, what got taken from him, and how he was in the wilderness for years.

I said to Gerald, 'we should write a book together about reinvention.' We were clearly on the same wavelength, because I didn't even have to explain the concept; he just said, 'yeah, I'm in.' He already knew.

I'm excited about this book. I think it's going to help a lot of people who are maybe being edged towards reinvention, or thrown into it, following the COVID-19 pandemic or any business and life challenges you may be facing. But it goes so far beyond that. I've already said it (and you'll read it again): reinvention is a vital part of business. To thrive, you have to be able to adapt, adjust, pivot, you need to be flexible and responsive and proactive, you need to spot trends and make fast decisions. You need to embrace change.

Who is the future you?

If you close your eyes and imagine the future, who are you? Knowing who you want to become, or how you want to grow, or the difference you want to make on the planet, will help you work out who you're going to reinvent yourself into.

When I finished university, I was meant to move to Australia and become an architect. If you don't know me, I can tell you now that it didn't happen. Not even a little bit. It turns out I did the right thing, and although the decision I made instead – to work in my parents' pub for five years – wasn't a winner either, I don't regret it. But I was going down someone else's road, because I didn't have options and I wasn't clear about who I was, or the career I wanted, or the life I saw for myself. If you don't have your own vision, someone else will make you part of theirs.

There are a lot of people out there like I was; maybe you're one of them. You might be living vicariously through other people because you feel like you don't have a choice. You might be getting sucked into someone else's dreams because their vision is stronger and clearer than yours. You may be lost. Stuck. Lonely. Comfortable.

Whatever your reason for reinvention, you've got the timing right. You might have had a serious illness or experienced a life-changing event. You may have been made redundant or just woken up one day wanting to do something different with your life. You may not need to reinvent yourself now but want to be prepared for when you inevitably do. Or maybe you want to keep reinventing yourself, disrupting yourself before someone else does.

Whether it's financial security, excitement, variety or something else you're looking for, I think it's really important to have the skills to be able to reinvent yourself before someone comes and pulls the rug out from under your life. Job security is a thing of the past; reinvention is a necessary, 'new normal' life skill. Some people discovered this a long time ago – just look at Madonna and Michael Jackson, who did this frequently to stretch their careers across decades.

Knowing how to take control of your own reinvention will give you a toolbox you can dip into forever, whether you're facing small challenges or massive obstacles.

How to read this book

This book is a bit different to my other books you might have read. It's the first time I've co-authored a book, and Gerald and I each bring our different perspectives forward to support you in your reinvention. Each chapter starts with Gerald sharing the story of his reinvention with you, and he then dives into the different aspects of reinvention. Each chapter ends with my perspective, and you can expect to get a lot of practical steps you can action in these parts, so get ready to work.

But this topic really lends itself to getting inspiration from other people's stories – hearing about people who turned failures into successes helps you believe that you can do it too. So you'll find case studies throughout the book too.

Can you think of a better time to be thinking about, planning and going through with a reinvention? It's easier than ever to reinvent yourself – you can set up an online business in minutes, you can get to market quicker, you can use social media to find communities and clients around the world. You can be a digital nomad, running your business from wherever your life takes you. It's no longer a world where people stay in their jobs for life; the world really is your oyster. And reinvention is all around us, it's become part of our culture. If reinvention used to be a luxury, perhaps now it is a necessity.

When it comes to reinvention, you don't have time to *get* ready, you need to *be* ready. At any time, in this new world order, you could be forced to reinvent or die. Gerald and I want to offer you a new life skill: the ability to reinvent yourself at a moment's notice. The confidence and skills to adapt, change and disrupt, to build the future career and life that puts you in control. Life by design, not by accident.

Rob Moore
The Disruptive Entrepreneur

Prologue to the First Edition
COVID-19: the biggest driver of change this generation has seen

It's impossible to write a book about reinvention without first talking about the biggest driver of change this generation has seen: COVID-19. Coronavirus was a game-changer, certainly in terms of business, employment and the economy, and probably for every aspect of our lives. It affected every single one of us in some way or another, me included.

COVID-19 threatened the entire global healthcare system. Governments around the world put measures in place to curb its spread and minimise the number of people who were affected; in the UK, that meant we were on lockdown. We had to stay at home as much as possible, and self-isolate if we were potentially infected or vulnerable. We had to keep a physical distance of six feet – about two meters – from each other. We were permitted to go out for essential shopping and once a day to exercise.

There was good reason for these measures. To date, there have been more than 43 million cases and, tragically, over 1.1 million deaths worldwide; the UK has seen more than 900,000 people infected and more than 45,000 people have died as a result.* People have lost parents, children, siblings, partners and friends. And for those who were infected, the course of the disease was unpredictable, with people ranging from being asymptomatic to needing ventilation in intensive care.

It was scary, and the fear manifested in some weird and wonderful ways. The first and biggest knee-jerk response was stockpiling: within a matter of days of the pandemic being announced, toilet paper was nowhere to be found. (One Australian newspaper, *The NT News*, even printed eight pages blank with cut-out lines for those in need.) Pasta and rice were flying off the shelves here, as were all manner of tinned goods. People were panicking because they didn't know what to expect. Uncertainty breeds anxiety.

* The latest numbers are available at coronavirus.jhu.edu.

We also saw outpourings of support and solidarity. Children drew colourful rainbows and stuck them in their windows. Regular rounds of applause for the NHS echoed down empty streets and donations helped keep the selfless and dedicated NHS staff equipped with the gear they needed to work safely.

But in addition to the heart-warming stories and strange shopping habits, there were some serious economic impacts, with long-term global repercussions. In the first two weeks of lockdown in the UK, 950,000 people applied for universal credit, according to the *Financial Times*. Across the pond, an estimated 22 million Americans lost their jobs in the space of a month – more than 13 percent of the workforce. That's a bigger relative impact on jobs than the Great Depression.

Predictions are of a double-digit decline in GDP in the UK. *But isn't a recession bad for business?* Yes, for many, it will be the end – we already saw a lot of businesses crumble because of the pandemic, including giants like Debenhams on the high street and Flybe in the air. In March 2020, 21,000 more businesses collapsed than in March 2019 – a 70 percent increase in failure. Unfortunately, many people went out of business in this situation; you may be one of them. But not everybody is going to suffer in the future, and I believe you can take action to make sure you don't.

There's opportunity in crisis

Despite the shutdowns, the recession may be one of the best opportunities you'll ever have to start a business. Many fortunes are made in times of recession; some of the world's most successful companies were born in recessions. Disney, Microsoft, FedEx, General Motors – all household names today – started during severe depressions and recessions. Why? These are the times when our needs are greatest, laid bare as the excess is stripped away, and that visibility lets entrepreneurial thinkers innovate and come up with companies that can help people.

This kind of crisis also levels the playing field by wiping out some of the big players. The old guard is replaced because new problems need to be solved in a new way. Fresh air is breathed into industries everywhere.

The opportunity lies in the combination of these two factors: businesses fail, leaving room for innovation. Lockdown led to a pent-up demand for the services we couldn't access (did you see any dodgy DIY haircuts?). People were crying out for personal touch (literally) and missing the things they were denied, like a meal with friends in a restaurant or a stress-relieving massage.

Many of the businesses offering these services were the ones shutting down because they had literally no turnover, no way of keeping the doors open. They were stung, and fear held people back from restarting after the end of lockdown. That provided an opportunity for those willing to take the risk – I saw people queueing down the street for a decent haircut when salons reopened!

Across the board, there won't be enough companies to cater for the pent-up demand in the aftermath of the crisis. A lot of people will take the view that it will be difficult to make money in the recession that's coming our way, so they won't invest, they won't start up. They will buy into the fear and the media-driven soundbites of hardship.

But it is the right time. There will be greater demand and less competition – a winning recipe for success. 'Be fearful when others are greedy and greedy when others are fearful', as Warren Buffet famously said.

There are huge opportunities everywhere. E-commerce businesses are seeing record sales, better than any Christmas they've seen before (and as someone who has worked through 54 Christmases in the jewellery business, minus a few while I was otherwise engaged, I can tell you that means huge turnover).

To be clear, I'm not talking about profiteering – it is completely wrong to sell a roll of toilet paper for a 5,000 percent mark-up. But there's absolutely nothing wrong with making a lot of money during hard times if you're helping people, if you're offering something the public want. That's capitalism, that's how our society works. And by making a profit, you can employ people, pay taxes and help get the economy running full speed again.

Video calling companies like Zoom exploded, and we weren't just using them for work; the world was having family meetings and pub quizzes on the platform. Home delivery enjoyed a renaissance and e-commerce shot up as an industry in response to massively increased demand.

The real death of the high street?

One place I think we might see a permanent change is the high street. For years, I've heard people warning of the death of the high street. Given how undesirable high street retail has been, I would often say that it's exactly where you should invest, take a risk, make some money.

Think about it: nobody wants in, so the rent gets driven down (in some places all the way to nothing). With significantly lower overheads, you have a bigger profit margin. Then it's just a case of figuring out what you can sell that doesn't put you in direct competition with the likes of Amazon.

But things have changed. One of the keys to success in reinvention, and in business and life more generally, is noticing, acknowledging and accepting change. Amazon became a behemoth during the pandemic, making $10,000 a second. People were only physically walking into shops for essential items, and even then, most preferred to order online.

Before COVID-19, a lot of people were getting into high street retail with the strategy of selling high-margin products and offering experience shopping – a glass of prosecco or a yoga class. But it doesn't add up; that's not the way to beat Amazon. They were trying to adapt to rival online, but they were not reinventing. It was too small, too incremental.

I think that you will be able to take shots on very low rent premises selling products and services that people want after the pandemic. This is what Rob does well: he buys property when the values are at the lowest point in the cycle. The biggest property crashes offer the best buying opportunities, like a closing-down fire sale.

If you're a hairdresser, you were probably inundated after lockdown, temporarily at least. People appreciated going out again, but that didn't mean they would eat out twice a week instead of once to make up for lost time. They wanted to try on clothes again, but they probably didn't double up on their shopping.

Nevertheless, I think there are a lot of things that people really missed and they'll want to do, see and buy more in the future. You have the opportunity to tap into that, to help service their need. Nowadays that can be simple – you can sell anything as a sole trader.

Your first step is to be positive. To see the opportunities and be prepared to take them. You just have to have your eyes wide open to SEE the opportunity. To be positive about the negatives.

Changing values

It's not just the world that has changed, it has also changed our values – changed what is most important to us now that the priorities have shifted. That's going to have an impact on your potential customers and your business opportunities, but also on you, your goals and your vision for the future.

We've lived a certain life that has become too comfortable or been completely turned upside-down by Coronavirus. It has changed our values. Many people were being competitive before the pandemic, on a treadmill of achievement, collecting material possessions and hoarding wealth for personal gain. Of course, there is still an element of that, which I think is largely down to fear, but there has been a shift in people's actions, needs and wants.

We have seen more consideration for others, more compassion and care. When I took my dog for a walk in mid-2020, I would see rainbow after rainbow in the windows of houses, supporting the National Health Service (NHS). We watched with pride and amazement as 99-year-old war veteran Captain Tom Moore walked 100 laps of his garden for his 100th birthday, and more than 1.5 million of us donated to his cause, helping him raise over £30 million for the NHS. Philanthropy has increased, and people are volunteering to help those in need.

We are also collectively more focused on family and friends, on people rather than things. For those of us locked down with our families, we appreciated the extra time with them (though of course it wasn't all roses – home schooling was hugely challenging for parents, for example). 2020 will go down in history as the year kids had their parents at home. And for those locked down in isolation, it was a reminder that connection is important, or even essential.

We are fortunate to have had technology on our side. FaceTime, WhatsApp video, Zoom, Google Hangouts, Houseparty and Facebook Messenger Rooms all let us speak to our loved ones when we needed that connection. And the numbers reflect just how significant that need was: video conferencing apps were downloaded 62 million times in one week in March 2020, with some apps being downloaded thousands of times more often than they were a few months before.

The lockdown also gave us a renewed appreciation of the outdoors and of our own health. It's certainly true that we can take things for granted and only miss them when they're gone. In the UK, we were allowed out once a day to exercise during the pandemic, and then we were limited to two kilometres from home. People embraced the situation, and I even noticed more people going for walks and enjoying their surroundings.

Gyms might have been closed, but there has been great opportunity in home workouts. Joe Wicks, The Body Coach, was keeping the UK fit with his 'P.E. With Joe' YouTube videos, live streamed at 9am UK time, and they were getting about 1 million views each. His following grew exponentially in the lockdown because he saw the opportunity, even before schools did. Apps like Peloton and devices like Fitbit helped people stay fit at home, and the fitness businesses that shifted their offerings online had a better chance of survival than those waiting to welcome people back in.

I think the restrictions combined with COVID-19 being a health crisis really brought health and fitness to the fore. People were scared of Coronavirus and the impact it could have on their health – we saw healthcare workers in masks and patients in quarantine bubbles, and in the end, many of us will have experienced the symptoms, spent time in hospital on ventilation or, tragically, lost loved ones to the infection.

We want to stay healthy; being proactive about that was one way to stay in control and beat the virus. Although some people have big fitness goals, the majority won't want to lift massive weights or run hundreds of miles. There is a growing market for innovative solutions that help us get fit or lose weight without too much effort. Yoga in your living room, bodyweight exercises in the garden, daily walks around the neighbourhood.

And then there's the mental health element, which remains critical. We saw increased anxiety and stress, and experts predicted a rise in suicides on the back of the pandemic, largely due to the rise in unemployment. The lockdown had some serious mental health impacts. People were lonely, not used to living without human contact. We are a social species and we literally respond biologically to touch – hugs can release hormones that make us feel happy.

There was also a lot of boredom, and while some people turned that to their advantage by picking up a new hobby or skill, others suffered a great deal, feeling lost and directionless. Kids were climbing the walls, and their parents were doing their best to 'crisis educate' them in very trying circumstances. This has been a shared trauma, and everyone is dealing with it differently.

Online products and services stepped in to help: the mindfulness app Headspace gave away free subscriptions to healthcare workers, and it saw a massive increase in downloads, as did other meditation and relaxation apps like Calm. People headed online to pick up hobbies, like learning a language on Duolingo or keeping their brains busy with a game of Scrabble with a friend.

I think the focus on personal health and more values-based consumption is taking over from the materialism we've been used to; people are less inclined to collect things. The panic buying we saw at the start of the pandemic highlighted the ridiculousness of our tendency to gather and hoard possessions – we have too much of everything, not just toilet roll. And now that people's cash reserves have dwindled, I think we'll become much more measured in how we interact with material things.

It makes me think back to how my mother used to cook. She would cook a chicken and it would last for days – the first meal, like a roast dinner, and the next day in a stir-fry, and she'd use the carcass to make a delicious soup. Nothing was wasted when she cooked. I think we'll go back to those values, and that's a good thing.

Reinvention during and after the pandemic

There will always be people innovating, whether that's online or physically, to try and improve people's mental and physical health, and COVID-19 provided an opportunity to tune into the changing needs and make money. And there's nothing wrong with that.

Yes, it was an extremely difficult time, it was a traumatic situation. We were living with this Sword of Damocles hanging over us. We didn't know what the future held, and there was a lot we couldn't control. But we all had to take a hit, and that varied – the suffering came in different forms, directly from the virus or indirectly through loss of earnings, loneliness and a whole range of other things that will continue to emerge in the aftermath. You need to be ready for these things.

If you embrace the change that's coming, you will benefit; carry on doing things the old way and you'll soon fall foul of the seismic shift in people's thinking and purchasing patterns.

For some people, right now that will mean falling on the system to survive. I don't think this is giving up. In the UK, we are fortunate to have a welfare system that looks after those who need it – and as taxpaying citizens, we are entitled to that help.

What I do think, though, is that it's important not to let yourself go on a downward spiral like I did. Sitting in bed all day will get you nowhere. The best things to be doing right now, whatever your situation, are staying positive, staying fit and staying alert. That means exercising your body and your mind – and reminding yourself that worrying will not help.

Regardless of how enticing it is, watching Netflix with a packet of crisps in your hand isn't going to make you happy. Self-gratification and short-term satisfaction don't achieve anything in the long run.

It may seem counterintuitive at first, but in your time of greatest need – and this is one such time for many people – helping others is a powerful way to thrive. Look at the people you know. Who seems to be keeping it together? Who is positive and proactive? I bet it's the people who are doing something to help – raising money, supporting people, volunteering to look after others.

I coped fine (I was doing self-isolation years before we had to, after The Speech, as you'll soon discover), but I took a hit, just like everyone else. I usually help people through my speeches and mentoring – I share my business expertise to support others on their entrepreneurial journeys. I had to adapt. During the lockdown, my calendar emptied; I lost my speaking gigs and the income that came with them.

But I'm not complaining, I continued to do everything I could to help people. I contributed to a US podcast series about how to recover, and it's expected to get 5 million downloads. And I wrote this book with Rob, in the hope that it helps you too.

For now, we'll wait to see what the long-term consequences are; I hope this book helps take the worry out of it for you. I've lost a £650,000 salary before (adjusted for inflation, that's £1.4 million); if this recession takes me down, I'll rise again – it wouldn't be the first time I've reinvented myself. I'm going to show you how to do it too.

CHAPTER 1
Ask Yourself WHY?

'Consonant please, Carol.' That's how the most stimulating part of my day started, as usual. I watched the British TV show Countdown every day, almost religiously. By now, though, after four long years, I had stopped trying to compete and started just passively watching the two contestants battle it out over alternate rounds of word and number puzzles.

The first contestant on this one particular day, an unemployed brainbox from somewhere on the south coast, got my heckles up. On paper, we were in the same boat – both unemployed, both with a full head of hair – but he had two big advantages over me: he was bordering on 20 years my junior, and he had just scored maximum points by finding a six-letter word hidden amongst the random selection of letters he had chosen. I only managed five.

As I sipped my tea, I could hear my wife Moira in the background, as busy as always. I had been sitting in bed for years (like I said, I was doing self-isolation before it was popular), and I knew my time would eventually run out, one way or another. She had been patient, supportive and loving through my – our – darkest days, but I had the impression that her patience was wearing thin; it was time for me to do something.

I knew there was no going back. How could anyone go back after tanking a billion-pound company with a few ill-chosen words? But in the depths of my depression (and, looking back, an unhealthy dose of feeling sorry for myself), I couldn't see a way to go forward. My reputation was in tatters, I didn't have a penny to my name, and I had no clear alternative path. It felt like a lost cause.

The clock was ticking. Literally, on TV – the day's returning champion had chosen his set of letters and the two were studiously looking for the best, longest words they could find. I didn't even try. The champion had a seven-letter word; the challenger took a punt on a dodgy seven-letter word too. The punt didn't work out and he ended up losing the game.

Whatever I was going to do at this point would have to be a punt. My very public downfall had effectively rendered me unemployable, and I was skint – I had no cash, no savings and no assets. I would have to dig deep – really deep – to find the courage and inspiration to get off the sofa, let alone reinvent myself.

Reinvention isn't always down to a moment, but it isn't always gradual either. In my case, it was a combination of the two – a disaster, followed by a slow descent, followed by a kick up the arse.

Not long after that particular episode of Countdown, Moira made it patently clear to me that my reinvention would be imminent, or she would be gone. I had a decision to make: would I continue to watch Countdown with a cup of tea, dwelling on my mistake day after day, agonising over the life I once had and what I had lost, or would I start again, create something new, reinvent myself?

It wasn't a choice at all, I knew I would have to take action somehow, find something within myself and make a change. I had lost almost everything; my family meant too much to lose them too. Like the Countdown contestant, I took the punt. But I won – I reinvented myself.

Learn from my mistakes – and successes

When Rob Moore asked me if I wanted to co-author a book with him, my thoughts went straight back to that moment – and all the others – sitting in bed watching TV, watching the hours, days, weeks, months and even years tick by. My wife saved me from still sitting there right now, and I'm eternally grateful for that kick up the arse. But had I read a book about someone else's journey, had I been given some tried and tested advice on reinvention, maybe it could have happened earlier and more easily.

That's what I want to give you. That's why I agreed to sharing my story again, and to diving into the different aspects of reinvention – what it is, why it happens and how to do it. In this book, you will come with me on my own journey of reinvention. I'll share the ups and downs, the mistakes and the wins. You'll feel the cringe but also the sparks of excitement that will lead you to your own path of reinvention.

What I went through was traumatic, devastating and deeply unenjoyable – I wouldn't wish it on my worst enemy. I certainly hope you don't ever have to experience anything like it.

And that's the point, you don't have to: you're reading this book, and if you keep reading, Rob and I will be your mentors through these pages, helping you navigate to a new life. You can learn from my mistakes, so you don't do the same. You can learn the lessons that took me years to learn in a fraction of the time. You can apply the tips and rules and approaches that I have developed, starting right now.

You can be and do whatever you want. The sky really is the limit. First, you have to figure out what that is – why do you want to reinvent yourself, and what do you really want from life?

What is your reason for reinvention?

It's comfortable on the sofa, isn't it? It's easy to put your feet up and open a packet of crisps, switch the TV on and line up a full-on binge of the latest Netflix series. And then the next one.

That's how easy it is to get into bad habits; just look at the Countdown habit I nurtured in the 90s. (I'm eternally grateful that Netflix and smartphones didn't exist when I was in bed.) And bad habits can very easily lead you into a place that is devoid of motivation and inspiration. That is where reinvention goes to die.

You need the push to change. The impetus to pivot. A reason to do something differently. The forces behind reinvention are external and internal. Both can give you the push you need to change, and it's important to understand what is motivating you before you take the next step.

External force – something that happens outside of you to push you to reinvent yourself.

None of us lives in a vacuum – we are all affected by our environment, the people around us, our work, our homes, the local and global economy, people's purchasing habits... the list goes on and on. Some external forces can act on you directly: perhaps you were made redundant or, like me, maybe you got sacked from leading a billion-pound turnover business after saying something daft in a speech. (No? Just me then?) Your office building or shop or warehouse might be sold from under you or collapse. You could fall ill. Your partner might want a divorce. External factors can force your reinvention indirectly too: new technology might be leading your industry in a different direction (just look what happened when the internet started) or a trend pushing you to change (think shoulder pad manufacturers in the 90s).

Internal force – something that happens inside of you to push you to reinvent yourself.

Your impetus for change might be coming from within – maybe you're bored of what you're doing or feel like you're not living and working in line with your values. You might have experienced something that awoke a need inside you to reinvent yourself – a near-death experience or losing someone you love, for example. Maybe you wake up and you're 25 years older, but you realise your life hasn't really moved forward and you say, 'enough is enough'. Maybe you had an experience so negative you never want to repeat it (like bullying) or something so exhilarating that you want more of it (time to become a skydiving instructor?). The change might be spurred on by your emotions – desire, fear, excitement, loneliness.

What's most likely is that if you're ready to reinvent yourself, there will be a combination of forces at play. Internal forces can easily be strong enough to push you to make a big change, but external forces rarely are; real change ultimately comes from within.

My major, very public, forced reinvention was down to a single external event on the surface, but in reality, that was just the start of it. What followed was years of soul-searching, psychological change and a lot of learning. For me, the external force was just the trigger: reinvention wasn't possible until the internal forces got into gear. I believe that is the case for everyone.

And reinvention isn't something that happens once. In fact, I think if you want to be successful in life, and especially in business, reinvention needs to be a constant in your world. You need to be in control of reinvention. You need to be able to implement it at a moment's notice.

I'm sharing the story of my downfall here, but that isn't the only time I reinvented myself. In fact, one of the reasons I have been successful in business from the start is that I was constantly shifting, changing, reinventing.

Before we look more closely at your reason for reinvention, let's examine one that many people share: COVID-19.

Coronavirus-induced reinvention

The COVID-19 pandemic literally changed the global economy. If you're employed, you may have been furloughed, made redundant or let go. If you're a sole trader, your work may have dried up. If you're a business owner, you may have had to make difficult decisions about your employees, or worse, been forced into administration or bankruptcy – like Hertz, Flybe and Gold's Gym.

The external changes brought about by the virus – the physical distancing measures, the rules around shop openings, the self-isolation guidance – may have pushed you to reinvent in order to survive. Whole industries have been ravaged – travel and hospitality were hardest hit, as we couldn't go anywhere with anyone. Others, like e-commerce, are booming, forcing reinvention in terms of expansion.

If this is the case, taking steps to reinvent yourself and your business might feel forced, frustrating, frightening, but if the alternative is failure, you're taking the step anyway. If your high street shop doors have been closed, perhaps you've opened a web shop. If you can't paint people's nails, perhaps you're posting how-to videos on YouTube and inviting people to take your online course. Necessity is the mother of invention.

If you've been pushed into standing (or lying) at the foot of the reinvention mountain, you will find strategies in this book that will help you reach the summit. And it starts with a single step.

This situation isn't just providing an external drive to change, it's also driving an internal one in many cases.

I see a lot of people spiralling in this situation, letting fear and anxiety cloud their judgement. It is particularly easy at a time like this to get into bad habits, because we're all creatures of habit. Those of us who are isolated at home are in this closeted, cocooned situation, and there may be little saving us from ourselves.

Without the gym, there might be less motivation to put on your sports clothes and work out at home. Without the office, there might be little reason to get out of bed, let alone get dressed in the morning. The potential for losing energy, drive and direction is huge.

We're also spending a lot more time with ourselves, feeling intensified emotions in all directions. Many people have stated that the infrequent highs are higher, and the frequent lows are lower. Everything seems more extreme.

If you've been feeling bored of the spreadsheets you're working on, you're probably overwhelmingly bored of them right now. If you have a passion for playing the piano but you don't usually have time to do it, the lure of the keys in the next room might be too much to bear.

Whether it's fear or boredom or passion or simply a dream, that internal drive might be stronger than ever in this situation, pushing you towards reinvention.

Whoever you are and whatever you are (or were) doing, I'm willing to bet that Coronavirus has forced you to make big changes, if not a full-on reinvention. It's disrupt-yourself-or-die time. Understanding what the underlying factors are can help you on your journey.

Finding direction

Coronavirus might be the biggest driver of change and reinvention for many people, but you could have an entirely different reason.

What is it? What's driving you? Is there something happening externally that is providing the impetus to make a change? Or is your inner voice shouting at you to do something?

Take some time to think carefully about this. Write a list of the external and internal forces that might be at play right now. Don't worry yet about what might be stopping you or why you can't implement these changes. Just write. Let it flow. This will help you work out which direction they're pushing you in, and whether that's where you want to go. I've got an exercise here that might help you.

For the first item on your list, write down how it's affecting you. Is it a positive or negative impact? Is it real or imagined? Which direction is it pushing you in?

Now write down three ways it could be pushing you to reinvent yourself. Make one of them quite small and simple, something you could imagine yourself doing, and make one of them outrageous. The idea here is to shake up your thinking a bit. Don't worry if they're not focused, you just want to get your imagination working.

Repeat this for all the things on your list.

Circle or underline recurring themes. Is there anything that surprises or excites you?

When you understand what's behind your need for reinvention, you can start to piece together where it's pushing you. And then you can decide if that's where you want to go.

When I left Ratners, I was forced to reinvent myself. It wasn't about me following my passion – I was born into the jewellery business (literally, my mother was working in the shop when she was pregnant with me) and it runs through my veins. But looking at what was driving the change I had to make, I realised I needed to step away from the business and do something new to get back on my feet.

Eventually I did come back to the jewellery business, in a second reinvention driven by my interests and the opportunities presented by the internet, which was still in relatively early days back then.

These are big changes – we often think of reinvention as being huge, significant, complete. But the seed I want to sow is that reinvention is also a state of mind and an ongoing process. Small changes can lead to big changes. Reinvention can be overwhelming, but it can start small. In the next chapter, we'll look at how change is an integral part of a successful business, and how embracing that can help you move forward in ways you might never have expected.

Rob: Check your mindset (you can do it)

We've all got examples of times we've had to change or chosen to change. And I think we've also all had times when we've been facing the drive to change but somehow been held back from doing anything about it. Doubt, anxiety, fear and habit have a lot to answer for.

Take the Coronavirus pandemic situation for example. There are people who knew they had to pivot their business, they had an idea of how, but they didn't do it, and instead they sat and watched the thing as it tanked. There are people who torture themselves for years, dreaming about turning their passion into a profession but not taking the first step to doing it. People who sit at their desks day in, day out, working in a crappy job they hate instead of listening to their inner voice, because they're 'too old' or 'not good enough'. Or because they have bills that need to be paid and mouths that need to be fed.

If I look back at my life so far, there's one example that I think brings a lot of issues you might be facing together. When I was in my mid-20s, I was a struggling artist, on the breadline, feeling sorry for myself and creating pieces about as dark as the music I was listening to (and that was dark). I was in £50,000 worth of consumer debt. I was working in my parents' pub, arguing with my dad. This was the life I'd decided was for me, the life I thought I deserved. It crept up on me over the course of seven years. It was supposed to be temporary, but I had become trapped in my own mind and my own fears.

Deep down, I knew I had to make a change, but I resisted it. Even when people told me I should look into property, I just shrugged off their suggestions and poured another beer. I'd had my chance, I thought, and I'd already reinvented myself as an artist after discovering I hated architecture. I didn't have the money. I didn't have the knowledge. I didn't have the confidence. I had to stick with it now, that was my lot in life. And I was happy in my misery (at least I had convinced myself I was), so I didn't have the motivation to catapult me out of it.

If you're considering a big change, toying with the idea of reinvention, I bet you've got all sorts of messages you're telling yourself. I want to address some of the things that are holding you back from taking the first step.

I'm too old. No you're not. I don't care if you're 30 or 90, you are never too old. If you're alive, you're young enough to reinvent yourself. Just look at Colonel Sanders: when he franchised Kentucky Fried Chicken, he was 62; he sold it 12 years later for $2 million (which is $16 million adjusted for inflation).

I failed in the past. Good. Because you need to fail in order to succeed (Gerald will dive deep into failure in chapter 3). Your past does not define who you are – the whole philosophy of reinvention is that you can be whoever you want to be, you can leave your past behind you and only take valuable lessons along for the ride. You can fail 100 times and still succeed. You are not what you have done, you are what you can do – and that is limitless.

I haven't got any money. Then use OPM – Other People's Money. There are so many ways to set yourself up in a new life or a new business without a penny to your name (and Gerald has a lot to say on this point). In property, there are loads of 'no money down' techniques that will get you off the ground and earning thousands in a short time. Almost every business that gets funding on Dragon's Den starts with no money; all they have is passion and a pitch.

I'm too shy/stupid/not confident. You are enough. I'll say it again: YOU. ARE. ENOUGH. You are good enough, smart enough, and you can learn to be more confident. You will never be happy with yourself if you're listening to those messages in your head, so it's time to start writing new ones.

My life is fine (not really). You will eventually be forced to change when you're motivated enough. 'If you're green you grow and if you're ripe, you rot'. Nothing stays the same. Standing still is moving backwards. Not growing is dying. It will creep up on you if you don't keep forcing yourself to grow. You can be in denial all you like, in the end that motivation will blast through and make you do something crazy. Instead, be honest with yourself about how you're feeling, look at reality in the cold light of day and make a conscious decision.

Whatever excuses your internal monologue is giving you, if they're not helping you, they're hurting you. It's time to reset those tapes – here's a simple method for doing that.

1. Notice when you're making an excuse. Literally stop yourself and say 'that's an excuse' – say it out loud (don't worry about the weird looks you'll get). The more you call it out, the more conscious you'll be of it and the less power it will have. This is called a pattern interrupt: you want to break your internal dialogue habits and change what you say to yourself.

2. Write a new script. What would help you more than those harmful excuses? Give yourself some power with three positive messages. Here are some examples: 'I can do anything I want!' 'I love [singing, property investing, writing, or whatever your passion is] and I will do it.' 'I am strong.' 'I am confident.' 'I am enough.' These affirmations are short, powerful statements you say to yourself (the mirror is optional). This is called a reframe. To turn the negative self-talk into a positive message. 'I can't' turns into 'How can I?'

3. Every time you catch yourself in one of your excuses (or any other negative self-talk, actually), choose one of your three affirmations and say it to yourself. Out loud, if you can. Say it over and over.

The more you do this, the more positive your self-talk will become and the more positive your attitude will become. As Gerald says, you need a positive attitude in order to spot opportunity, especially in a challenging situation. Doing this will give you a good mental foundation for the reinvention you want.

Famous reasons for reinvention

Let's look at a few companies that reinvented themselves and look for the reasons behind their reinvention.

1. New blood: Nintendo

In 1889, Japanese entrepreneur Fusajiro Yamauchi founded Nintendo Koppai, a 'Hanafuda' – a card shop. It was actually a lot more daring than it sounds – the Japanese government had banned people from having playing cards, because of their link to gambling. But Yamauchi's card games were allowed, and his shop flourished so much so that he opened a second store in Osaka and created more card games.

When he died, he left the company to his son-in-law Sekiryo Kaneda, who expanded the business, which was already the country's biggest card business, to include Western cards and wider distribution.

Kaneda retired in 1949 and passed the company on to his grandson Hiroshi Yamauchi, who was 21 at the time, then died shortly thereafter. Yamauchi didn't just continue to grow the company; over the next 63 years, he transformed it. He was concerned about the limited market, so got to work testing other products and services, including instant rice, taxis and toys.

After distributing the Magnavox Odyssey in Japan, the world's first home video game console, Nintendo released the first of its own consoles, the TV-Game in 1977. Just a few years later, the company got its big break in the arcade, with Donkey Kong, in which a very early Mario appeared. In 1985, the NES console hit the US market, changing the way we play games forever.

2. Culture: National Geographic

I'm sure you're familiar with the iconic yellow cover of the *National Geographic* – a magazine packed full of high-quality articles and stunning photographs related to the natural world. The National Geographic Society published the first issue in 1888, and for more than a century, it was a mainstay of the magazine world.

But in the 1990s, it started to age – the younger generation was rejecting it, and sales plummeted. Having seen other publications fold, CEO John Fahey didn't want to kiss the *National Geographic* goodbye, so he reinvented it as a multimedia publication that shares content on TV and social media.

The company has flourished, largely due to a highly successful television channel showing nature documentaries and reality TV shows. Success in part has been down to the leadership of major shareholder Rupert Murdoch.

Today, the company has a huge audience on social media, including 27 million followers on Twitter, more than 120 million on Facebook, and 137 million on Instagram.

3. Changing technology: Western Union

After the first telegraph message was sent from Washington, D.C. To Baltimore in 1844, entrepreneurs across America started laying telegraph lines to take advantage of the new technology. One of those early adopters was the then New-York and Mississippi Valley Printing Technology Company – now Western Union.

The plan was a huge success, and by 1929, the company was making a profit by sending more than 200 million telegrams a year. But when was the last time you sent a telegram? Other technologies superseded the telegram, and Western Union kept up: they offered a fax service from 1935, launched a communications satellite in 1974 and started an early email service in 1982.

With an eye on fast-changing technology, Western Union had diverse interests: the company started its wire money transfer business as early as 1871, and today, it's still the largest of its kind, with 500,000 agents in 200 countries.

4. Anger: Berkshire Hathaway

Business isn't all cold, rational decisions; we can get hot-headed, especially when the pressure's on. This can spell disaster, but it can also have excellent results. One iconic story is that of legendary investor Warren Buffet and his holding company Berkshire Hathaway.

The company started life in 1888 as the Hathaway Manufacturing Co., which opened a textile mill in 1927. It merged with Berkshire Fine Spinning Associates in 1955 and became Berkshire Hathaway. When the textile industry started shrinking in the early 1960s, Warren Buffett, a driven 30-something entrepreneur, was buying cheap stock and selling it back to the company for a profit. It was going well until the CEO agreed a price with Buffett and then tried to lowball him on the sale.

Buffett was angry, and he decided to get rid of the owners by buying a majority stake in the company. Two decades later, he cut off the textile business and used the company as a holding for his investments. Today, Buffett has a net worth of over $80 billion.

5. Inspiration: Lego

It's hard to think of a child who doesn't own at least one Lego set. One of the most popular toys today, Lego has always been developed through inspiration.

Danish carpenter Ole Kirk Christiansen started making wooden toys in 1932, and named his company Lego two years later, based on the Danish *leg godt* – 'play well'. Christiansen started making plastic toys in 1947 and got inspiration for a new kind of toy when he received a sample of Kiddicraft bricks from the UK. The bricks looked strikingly like the Lego design Christiansen came up with and took to market as 'Automatic Binding Bricks'.

In the mid-1950s, Christiansen's son Godtfred took a leadership role in the company and developed the bricks into a system, bringing in the modern design in 1958. Since then, Lego has introduced giant bricks for younger kids (Duplo), minifigures and endless themed sets, from iconic movie models like the Star Wars Death Star and Harry Potter sets to Women of NASA and dinosaurs. Lego now has various categories – Technic, Junior, City, Creator, Architecture… – and the headquarters is such a creative inspiration it has featured in its own documentary.

CHAPTER 2
Embrace Change

I want to take you back in time (if you can remember this far): it's 1986, Peter Gabriel and Madonna are blasting through boom boxes, hair is getting wilder, skirts shorter and shoulder pads bigger. And I'm a rockstar of the business world. I'm living the high life, hanging around with business celebrities, getting interviewed all over the place, making loads of money and absolutely loving the adrenaline rush of business acquisition.

When I took over as Managing Director of Ratners, the company was worth £13 million; by 1986, I was well on my way to taking it to £1 billion turnover. We were taking more money per square foot in Ratners shops than any other retailer in Europe, and our shares were the highest performing – they had shot up from £0.35 when I took over to about £4.

However you cut it, Ratners was a roaring success. I had built the world's largest, most profitable jewellery business, and I'd done it with a very simple formula – one that nobody else had considered.

The jewellery business had become tailored to the older demographic – in the past, they had been the people with the money. So products, shop design and marketing were all aimed at those people. It meant everything had a more prestige feel to it, more upmarket. But to the customers of the 80s, it felt stuffy, pompous, inaccessible. The world had changed, but the jewellery shops had stayed the same.

The biggest change was that there was a lot of disposable income among young people: it was the 16-to-24-year-olds who had the cash. And that was great, because young people buy jewellery: they fall in love and get married, so they needed engagement rings, wedding rings, diamond necklaces and so on.

I could see the change, and I wasn't in any way afraid of it or opposed to it; I embraced it. The shift in demographics came together with a change in politics, which made growing a company much more possible: in the mid-80s, Margaret Thatcher was Prime Minister, and she was very sympathetic to business.

I was also spending time with a couple of close friends who had a big influence on me – I'll share more about that in a later chapter – and their advice and example helped put me on a path towards acquisition that grew Ratners into a company that's now thriving in the US and worth about £13 billion.

Growing through acquisition

The changing demographics, favourable politics and encouraging friends came together and put a fire under me: I started acquiring companies left, right and centre. Acquisition can be a solid business strategy across industries, but it was particularly important in jewellery. Why? There's no branding on the products. There's no logo on an eternity ring or a silver bracelet. The value was in the name above the door – and it can be very valuable indeed.

Look at the fashion business, for example. Companies like Armani and H&M have been known to buy some of the same product from the same supplier, but because of the value of the Armani brand, the products sold under that name carry a premium.

It's the same in jewellery; people feel much more comfortable buying from a well-known brand. So my strategy was to buy all the top brands. At the time, that was the likes of Leslie Davis, Ernest Jones and, most importantly, H. Samuel.

When we acquired H. Samuel (which effectively involved a long game of cat and mouse, in and out of the press), we put the same product in those shops. The difference was we could sell three times as many because the name was so powerful.

By the end of the acquisitions, we owned 50 percent of the jewellery market, and I was ready to crack America. Our shares were at just over £4, and to raise the capital to start acquiring stores in the US, I sold shares at their expected future value of £6, knowing we'd reach that in a few years. (Little did I know those shares would instead plummet as a result of The Speech.) I bought 125 shops that were doing fantastically well and just expanded. When somebody comes up with a good idea and it works, the next stage is expansion, taking it to the next level.

A simple concept that embraced change

Why did Ratners become so successful? The concept I pushed within that context of young people with disposable income was discounting.

I was ambitious in the 80s, and I was very eager to find a solution to the static profits we had been seeing when I took over the leadership of Ratners. Fashion and electronics businesses were booming, and I wanted to take jewellery in the same direction.

I looked carefully at our products, including our range of Seiko watches, which weren't moving spectacularly well. I spoke to a Seiko sales rep who visited one day and mentioned my concern. He was quite happy with sales – he told me we were about average, at 300 units per Ratners store.

At the time, he told me, our competitors (who I hadn't yet acquired) were in the ballpark – Ernest Jones were selling 150, H. Samuel 250, and Beaverbrooks (which I never acquired) 500. I was dejected. Then he added 'not counting Green and Symons, which takes our end-of-line product; they're averaging 3,000.'

To me, it was a no-brainer: that's where the money was. I went to the shop immediately and all the watches were half price. The answer was in discounting. While the usual suspects fought it out over the same products at full price, this company was leaving us all for dead, selling ten times our volume, by taking the products we didn't want. And why? Pride? Image?

When you follow the profit, you find what the customers are looking for. It was so obvious to me that this was a sign of changing demand: people wanted discounted watches; they weren't interested if they were the latest models. And the same was true of our other product lines too. The days of unmarked jewellery and uninviting shops were numbered.

People immediately turned their noses up: it was abhorrent to them; it was going down-market. And besides, it wasn't innovative, they said, everyone's offering discounts. I might not have been an innovator, but I could see where the market was going, and I wasn't afraid to make a change. And it was a dramatic change: Ratners started taking a more affordable, price-driven, aggressive marketing approach, and it really kicked me off.

The first thing we did was make the shops more inviting and accessible. We ditched the chandeliers and the three-piece suits. We played pop music in the shops (can you believe it?!). We moved the more affordable products like earrings and necklaces to the front of the windows, and the expensive rings went to the back. We priced things clearly, we put posters up with discounts and offers – we started selling on impulse.

This dramatic change is what started the glory days of Ratners – the profit, the acquisitions, the success. Today's world might be very different, but the same principles apply: you have to keep your eyes open and be ready to adapt to change, or you'll go down with the rest.

Today's world runs on change – and that's terrifying.

> *'Your life does not get better by chance, it gets better by change.'*
> *– Jim Rohn*

Like it or not, we are living in fast-changing times: things have never been shifting at a faster rate. I think that has a lot to do with technology – not only what it enables us to do, but how it's changed our expectations of what's possible. The internet has revolutionised retail and every other industry, and social media and global interconnectedness has altered our lives beyond recognition. People today are more distracted, less attentive and less committed, in every sense.

Yet change is right up there with fear of public speaking and death as one of the things that people fear the most. Think about how stressful it was the last time you moved house or changed jobs. It's human nature to seek the familiar. We like routine, we like comfortable surroundings and situations, we like to spend time with people we know. We like our lives and the world to run like clockwork and be predictable, so we know what is going to happen and when. That's why in England you eat fish and chips on a Friday. That's why television scheduling works, why we're comforted when we hear the key in the door when our kids get home from school. Everything's hunky-dory, everyone's happy.

But in business that is complete and utter disaster. If you carry on being that same person who runs the same business in the same way from the same office, you're not going to make any money. Your competitors will change and leave you behind. Your customers will grow up, evolve and move away from your brand.

Reinventing yourself is change, and it's something you have to embrace.

Take employment as an example. At the risk of making myself sound old, back in my day, people would follow in their parents' footsteps – they might be doctors or butchers or carpenters, for example – and they would have a lifelong job. It wasn't at all uncommon for someone to work at a company for 40 years and then retire with a pension.

Businesses would be 'Smith & Sons', it would be a given that they would pass from parent to child. Look at me – I took over Ratners from my father, who took it over from his father. The same was happening across the industry – H. Samuel was run by the Edgar brothers who passed the business on to their son, and Ernest Jones was the Weinsteins.

That might sound comforting, all that stability, or it might bore you to tears. Either way, it's a thing of the past: life is different now. Most people don't follow in their parents' footsteps. Their careers last five years, not 50. You can earn more money by moving jobs and companies than by staying put in undying loyalty.

We're seeing the rise of the digital nomads – people who travel the world working from their laptops and smartphones. Micro-retirements are giving people extended holidays, a rest from the thrust and grind of sipping piña coladas while they photoshop their latest Instagram photos.

That's how it looks to many people, but the reality is that the younger generation, the people entering their careers now, are facing a different set of problems. They are problems we're all increasingly facing as the world continues to change, and they are presenting us with obstacles we've never had to overcome before.

That idyllic digital nomad life is set against a backdrop of fear and uncertainty. When is the next gig coming in? Will I be able to pay my rent next month? What do I do about the trolls on social media threatening my brand?

It's the same for employment, which is transient today. People rarely stay in a job for more than a couple of years – globalisation makes it easy for companies to hire people anywhere, fast-changing business means jobs aren't safe because whole companies may be at risk, and loyalties have shifted from companies to people, which means when one person leaves a job, they often take others with them.

But the big factor I think is really positive is that people's expectations have changed, and they are taking more control. They don't want to be a cog in the machine. They want to have autonomy, they want to be treated with respect, they want to earn on merit and make a difference. Those things go beyond salary. There's a huge amount of research that shows job motivation doesn't come from bonuses, but rather from these less tangible factors.

That doesn't make it easy; the uncertainty can have a staggering effect. I see it first-hand with my kids. When they say they're going to move jobs, my immediate reaction is to be terrified – I think I'm more worried for them than I am for myself most of the time. I think, *why would you leave a perfectly good job and start a new one, where you'll be on probation? Why step into the unknown willingly?*

My son was a secondary school teacher, and he had a safe, solid job. He did some local radio DJing on the side, unpaid, and he loved it. Then suddenly he was offered a job doing the travel for a company that supplies the audio to a lot of radio stations. It was part-time, so on paper he was giving up a full-time job for a part-time one. And you know what? He made the right decision. He's since picked up a lot of extra days, and he's much happier – he loves what he's doing.

My daughter worked in events for *The Economist*, which I thought was the best place you could ever work, but actually, she was going nowhere. She completely changed course, and she's now working for a company that does peer-to-peer lending – and she's doing phenomenally well.

Staying put is the soft option. A lot of the worst career moves are staying where you are too long. You can have a great job, a safe position with a high salary, but if you're not happy in it, you have no real prospects at all. What is money if you're miserable? I can tell you it's nothing.

Look at the successful people you know; they have not stayed put. They have not taken the safe option. They have gambled.

It's the same in business. I can almost guarantee that you won't be passing your business down to your children; at least not the way it looks today. Looking at the jewellery businesses that are still going today, there's no family connection anywhere near the big players. It goes beyond trends; nepotism isn't something people will put up with. Today the world of work runs largely as a meritocracy – it's people who perform well, sell more, and go above and beyond who progress.

Fighting the fear of change

So change is essential, in business and in life; more than that, it's inevitable. But it's still scary. For a lot of people, risking the security that comes with a full-time job, especially if they have a mortgage and other commitments, is too much. And the fear of the unknown can be overwhelming.

How can you embrace change rather than running from it?

Over the years, people have pointed out that I don't have that fear. Certainly when I was running Ratners, people were shocked by the risks I would take and the dramatic changes I would make without batting an eyelid. I think this is a trait I got from my father, and it's probably one I've passed on to my children. To me, it's the essence of entrepreneurialism, and it's something you can start to embrace if you routinely follow five simple (but not easy) steps.

1. Accept the inevitability of change. I'm constantly changing, constantly in the process of reinvention. Anybody who thinks that they can just sit back and repeat the same thing and the business or the success will come to them is wrong. Accept that change is constant and will happen. (If you find change traumatic, there's a whole process to get to the acceptance part, but for now, let's leave it at the goal.)

2. Observe reality. Once you've accepted that change is inevitable, it's easier for you to see reality the way it is, because you will recognise that you may have a filter of expectation over things. Keep your eyes open and try to spot things as they start to shift. That way, you'll be able to spot change on its way.

3. Make the connection. With a view of what's changing and what may be to come, you can start to make connections: what does the change mean for you? What impact will it have on your life and your business? How can you pivot to be successful in the new situation?

4. Take action. JFDI, as Rob says. It's easier said than done, of course, but sometimes you have to jump in (see chapter 6). The key thing to remember is whatever decision you're making, it is highly unlikely to be a rest-of-your-life decision. You don't write the whole book in one go, you do it chapter by chapter. You are taking action for this chapter, this scene, maybe just this sentence. Very few things can't be undone.

5. Repeat. Every day. Over and over. The more you do it, the more you'll get used to it and embrace it in your life.

Change is inevitable, and it will often be out of your control, but you can get a head start on it by taking these steps. Even if you're slightly ahead of or right on a change or trend, being speedy (not hasty, there is a difference) will help you weather any storm.

Rob: what is reinvention?

When I'm working on a new project, I ask you – my readers, my community – what you want out of it. I ask questions about what things mean to you, about how you have done things in your own life, what you want to learn. I ask for your struggles, challenges and desired solutions. You know far better than me what you want.

When Gerald and I agreed to write this book together, I asked you what we should call it. Now just to give you a bit of context, the world was still laughing after the whole Boaty McBoatface debacle (Google it if you don't know what this is, it's hilarious), so funny titles were fair game. And my groups being as radically honest as they sometimes are, I was in for a treat.

I had posted a few options for the title in a poll on Facebook, and an unexpected contender shot up to second place:

Same shit, different you.

As much as it made me laugh, there's no way I was going to put that on the cover. (Books with swear words on them have been done to death, so you can all f*** off.) But looking back over the poll, I wanted to talk about it here, because I think it's actually an important point.

This title implies that reinvention is a process of changing yourself while everything else remains the same. That the world around you is static and you are dynamic. That it requires energy and effort to change yourself in the calm waters that surround you.

That might well be the case sometimes, but it's not the kind of reinvention I had in mind when we came up with the concept for this book.

To me, reinvention is about moving with the times, adapting and adjusting, evolving or dying, thriving not surviving… to use a word that's become seriously popular during the lockdown, it's about PIVOTING.

In my model for change, acceptance is a vital step (there are six – disruption, denial, resistance, acceptance, evaluation and implementation – which we'll return to in chapter 4). Once you've embraced change, you can move on – there's a whole universe of reinvention open to you.

Ways to reinvent yourself

Reinvention isn't about having a midlife crisis. It's not just for people on the run, hiding from the authorities. You can choose to reinvent yourself at any moment and for any reason; I've reinvented myself many times in my life. I went from architecture student to pub landlord. Pub landlord to artist. Artist to property investor. Property investor to entrepreneur. Entrepreneur to public speaker, social media creator, podcaster; and more recently I've turned our live events company into an online events company.

Reinvention sounds radical, and it can be. Some people have literally, physically changed themselves and their entire lives, like Caitlyn Jenner. Some have reinvented their professional lives – Gerald is a great example, and he's sharing his story throughout this book. Some reinvent smaller aspects of their lives – it could be their relationship, or their expertise, or their appearance. Then there are companies that reinvent entire industries, like Virgin, Netflix, Amazon and Apple.

As Gerald has explained, the motivation for reinvention can be internal or external or a combination of both. I agree that we're going to see a huge wave of reinvention coming after the Coronavirus pandemic. When we were in lockdown, I did an episode of my podcast 'The Disruptive Entrepreneur' about 'reinvention' being my word of the crisis (along with 'pivot', 'since COVID' and 'Coronacoaster!).

So many traditional businesses and ways of living just don't work anymore. If you want to thrive, not just survive, you can't wait to be great. You have to reinvent YOURSELF. Some people are using the word pivot, but in this case, I think it's stronger than that.

In my business, we have had to become a completely online training company, virtually overnight. When it became clear that the situation was going to continue, we realised we wouldn't be able to do face-to-face courses anymore, and we created various new online courses very quickly.

Three of the courses and masterminds we created are on e-commerce, because we could see that retail was one of the hardest hit industries and there was a need for reinvention there. But more than that, there is a huge opportunity around e-commerce today. We've seen crazy growth, not only for Amazon and Jeff Bezos but also for other sites, like Etsy and Shopify. We're seeing companies switching fast and making a fortune. Proactive, entrepreneurial, solution-focused people who can cut out the noise and the pandemic of fear are starting businesses.

On the face of it, moving from bricks-and-mortar retail to online sales might not seem like a leap, but look at what's involved. You have to learn and adapt to completely new systems. You have to reach your audience in a new way, which means new ways of advertising, of branding, of communicating. Imagine a shop that sells scented candles; the smell of the place could be its biggest selling point, but they don't make scratch-and-sniff computers (yet… can you imagine?!). How do you appeal to your customers through the screen?

This isn't progress, it isn't iterative. It is drastic and fast and vital, which is why I think the strength of the word reinvention best suits this situation.

Embrace change and anything is possible

As Gerald wrote, fear of change is understandable, normal. In fact, I'd go further and say it is vital for survival. It serves as well as stunts. I want to add a side-note to his steps to embracing change: turn your fear into excitement.

When you're afraid, it's the ancient part of your brain in action, making you freeze or fight or flee from the sabre-toothed cat that's about to attack you. We take comfort in the familiar because familiar is safe. In unfamiliar surroundings and situations, that old mechanism takes over and gives us a dose of adrenaline, the 'fight or flight' hormone.

As society has evolved, and previously dangerous situations have become safer, our brains have not evolved as fast, and we get 'triggered' into these fear-based emotions in a myriad of mundane, or at least non-threatening, situations, like public speaking. You're not going to die from it, but you often feel like you will. (In fact, I believe it ranks above fear of death!)

The quicker and quicker the world evolves, the harder it will be for the brain to catch up and the more situations will trigger us. If we are not aware of this, if we are not managing this fear, if we are not contextualising the situation to the modern world, we will experience more and more fear and become more and more resistant to change.

There's a great lesson we can learn from professional athletes about this: watch any pre-race interview; when the interviewer (predictably) asks the athlete if they're nervous, more often than not they will answer 'no, I'm excited.'

Excitement is the other side of the fear coin. Many scientists say fear and excitement are very similar emotions. In fact, TV host and author Mel Robbins believes they are the same. With practice, you can turn the tingly, uncomfortable feeling of fear into the tingly, enjoyable feeling of excitement. And then the world is your oyster.

Change brings with it even more opportunity than no change at all. There is no opportunity in 'the same as before'. There is only opportunity in NEW. New is entangled with 'hard' and 'scary'. Opportunity is often hidden in plain sight. By turning your fear into excitement and embracing change, you can see the opportunity and do anything. Anything.

Want to learn a new skill? You can. Start a business? You can. Move to a different country? You can. Get fit? You can. Get rich? You can.

In fact, you *already have* in your life, many times over. Perhaps you've just forgotten or not given yourself the credit for it. You are highly adaptable. Perhaps humans are the most adaptable of all species; which means you are too.

I want to spark your excitement with a little visualisation exercise. For each of these areas of your life, think about one or more ways you could reinvent yourself. Write them down.

- Work – your business or your job

- Finance – your assets and cash

- Romantic relationship – your significant other (or others... I'm not here to judge)

- Friendship – the people you choose to spend time with

- Family – the people you're most closely connected to

- Home – where you live

- Body – your physical self

- Mind – your knowledge and mental capacity

- Spirit – your spiritual self, your essence and values

Do any of these make you excited? Choose up to three and dive deeper into the possibilities – just the result at this stage, ignore the how. What would your life be like if it happened? Play around with it – you could create a vision board or write a letter from your future self. Immerse yourself in that change. How does it feel?

Perhaps you could use redundancy or apathy in your job to start your own business. Perhaps you could use lockdowns and quarantines to speak more to family and friends on the phone. (How great were the Zoom quizzes and Friday nights in – in-in, not out-out – on Zoom?!) Perhaps you could start home workouts with Joe Wicks and save on gym memberships you never actually use. Perhaps you could go on long walks instead of having to be carried to the fridge.

Are you ready to embrace change?

Apple

On 25 March 2019, Apple held a special event at the Steve Jobs Theater. The glint of 1,000 backlit devices preceded a colourful retro-style movie intro that introduced an unprecedented launch. Apple CEO Tim Cook walked onto the stage, his hands together in front of his plainly dressed body, thanking the audience emphatically. He went on to announce a range of new offerings.

For the first time in nearly a decade, iPhones had accounted for less than half of the company's revenue, and Apple was once again at a moment of reinvention. None of the products announced at the event were Apple devices; all were services in competition with tech giants like Netflix, Amazon and Google.

1.   Apple TV+: Apple's streaming service.

2.   News+: Access to hundreds of publications.

3.   Arcade: 'A gaming service unlike any other' that provides access to story-based games.

4.   Card: A credit card, without the need for a bank.

Putting a computer in every home

This isn't the first time Apple has reinvented itself. When Steve Jobs, Steve Wozniak and Ronald Wayne founded the company in 1976, they envisioned a personal computer that would give people access to the technology at home. Priced at $666.66, the Apple I was a huge hit, as was the Apple II that followed; the company grew at 533 percent, from annual sales of $775,000 in 1977 to $118 million in 1980. That December, Apple went public – and within a day, the stock had skyrocketed, creating 300 millionaires.

That wasn't success for Jobs; he had a bigger vision. Apple went on to launch the Macintosh – the world's first personal computer without a programming language, giving even more people access. The next year, Apple took a role in the publishing industry with a desktop publishing program called PageMaker.

By the end of the 1980s, lower priced PCs on the market had started cutting into revenue, so Apple launched a series of lower-cost Macintoshes – the Classic, the LC and the Ilsi. Then, in 1991, having achieved the goal of putting computers in homes, Apple set out to put them on our laps: they launched the PowerBook, setting the standard for all laptops that followed.

Apple survived a tumultuous period between 1991 and 1997, with flops, tech fails, lawsuits and an ousted CEO. Interestingly, they had a series of failures that were badly timed brilliant ideas, several of which would later become central in their offerings: digital cameras (now a major selling point of the iPhone), portable CD audio players (the forerunner to the iPod), speakers (AirPods), TV appliances (Apple TV), video consoles and an online service called eWorld. It just goes to show that timing is everything.

The rise of personal devices

In the late 1990s, Apple turned the tables once again. Success returned with new operating systems, the iMac and the return of Steve Jobs. iMovie, Final Cut Pro and Garage Band further embedded Apple in the creative industries, leaving business to Microsoft and the PCs.

Apple sold more than 100 million iPods in the six years following its 2001 launch, again setting the standard for mp3 players across the market. Then in 2007, Apple solidified its position as a leader in consumer devices, with the historic launch of the iPhone.

The company invited others to share its success in 2008, with the launch of the App Store, which let third-party developers sell apps for the iPod Touch and the iPhone and, after 2010, the iPad.

Every year since has seen an upgrade in each of Apple's devices, incorporating more and more features led by consumer demand. The latest iPhone at the time of writing – the iPhone 11 – has a dual camera system supporting professional photography and high-quality videography; it's made of touch glass; it's waterproof up to two meters for half an hour; it has a long-life battery; and it has the fastest chip ever seen in a smartphone.

In 2016, Apple topped the Forbes 500 list as the highest revenue generating company in the tech world. As of 2019, Apple had a revenue of $260 billion. All thanks to a rich history of reinvention.

CHAPTER 3
Invite Failure

'Good afternoon, Mr. President, Your Royal Highness, ladies and gentlemen. And thank you, Mr. President, for asking me to address such a prestigious audience.'

I was nervous. I'm always nervous when I speak, and I think it's a good sign; the alternative is arrogance, and when you reach that point, you might as well give up. Standing on stage at the Royal Albert Hall inspires an overwhelming sense of awe – it's a beautiful, iconic theatre, and as I walked up the steps to the stage, I imagined those who had gone before me. Sir Winston Churchill, the Dalai Lama, Tina Turner…

I looked out over the crowd. I was speaking to the Institute of Business Directors at their Annual Convention, on the 23rd of April 1991. A lot of men in grey suits. It wasn't the first time I'd spoken at one of their events, and I was well prepared for the speech. I had written and rewritten it in the weeks leading up to the evening, and I'd even asked other people for their input.

The Convention was on the theme of quality, choice and prosperity, and it gave me a great in for a few jokes directed at the people who had criticised my approach, who had condemned me for going 'down-market'. I continued:

'Well, this has been quite a difficult recession. In previous recessions, manufacturing took the brunt, but this time, the recession's main victims are the high street retailers. This recession is high street-led. Now as jewellery is a luxury purchase, you might think that we at Ratners would be suffering more than most, but we're not. We're not on the crest of a wave either. But we are coping.'

I went on to talk about the profits we had reported the previous day – £120 million. Quite a change from the £350,000 loss we had reported just eight years before. I was going to share our story in the speech, highlight our disruptive approach and how going against the grain had helped make us successful. I linked our brands to the different themes of the conference: our diamond specialist Zales represented quality, H. Samuel quality and Watches of Switzerland prosperity.

Then I made a joke that a set of earrings we sold was 'cheaper than an M&S prawn sandwich but probably wouldn't last as long.'

The hall was erupting in laughter, and I was loving it. I live to make people laugh, and my jokes were going down brilliantly. I talked about the teapot we sold for two quid, the not-so-tasteful imitation coffee table book, complete with fake antique dust, that had made us a fortune.

In my memory, what came next is frozen in time.

'We also do this nice sherry decanter, it's cut glass and it comes complete with six glasses on a silver-plated tray that your butler could bring you in and serve you drinks on, and it really only costs four pounds 95 pence. People say to me, how can you sell this for such a low price? I say because it's total crap.'

When I think about it, the laughter echoes around in my head just like it did around the hall that night.

At the time, I felt invincible. They were laughing! I love making people laugh, that's why I had written the jokes into the speech in the first place – and kept them in, despite my assistant's recommendation to take them out.

At the time, I was blissfully unaware of what had started to germinate as I stood there on the stage: the rumblings of what ultimately became a PR disaster of epic proportions.

Despite the audience responding positively to my speech, and laughing a lot, the press picked up on my 'crap' comment and a couple of other jokes and pulled me through the headlines in the days and weeks that followed. As it turned out, as much as people liked being able to buy less expensive products, they certainly didn't like it being pointed out to them.

I hadn't thought about that; in truth, I had intended the jokes to be self-deprecating, certainly not aimed at insulting customers, as the press had implied. There were claims that I had made fun of customers because I thought it was a private event. That was never the case – I had given the press a copy of my speech before I ever got on stage.

Public enemy number one

The press had a field day. Only it lasted a lot longer than a day. The headlines screamed 'Gerald Crapner'. They took my jokes, which were admittedly in bad taste, out of context and used them to burn every shred of connection our customers had with the Ratners brand.

The company was in big trouble. By February 1992, Ratners was £122.3 million in the red, and the papers were revelling in the news that 330 shops were being forced to close. I recruited a new chairman to guide us back into calm waters, and he quickly decided that would involve guiding me into his office and firing me.

I lost everything. I had ploughed almost every penny I made back into shares as I built the company, and those shares went from 425 pence to 2 pence practically overnight – the biggest drop ever seen on the London Stock Exchange. What's more, they came with massive tax bills. By 1992, I was in a negative equity situation – penniless, jobless and hopeless.

Invite failure

People ask me if I regret The Speech. What a stupid question, of course I bloody regret it! Given a choice, I would opt for any number of different mistakes in its place. But it's the mistake that has brought me here, with you, dear reader.

You see, we all need to make mistakes. Failure is what drives success. I'm sure this isn't news to you, but don't gloss over it – now is the time to dig into what it means, what it looks like, what it feels like, and apply it to your life.

Of course I regret The Speech, but that doesn't mean I avoid failure. In fact, the path I took to success today looks more like a random selection of slippery steppingstones across a raging river than a nice straight path across a peaceful meadow. And thank god, because that would have bored me to death.

I really believe that the reason I've been successful is that I've had so many failures. You can compare it to being a footballer who misses a goal. Whether it was a long shot you missed, or the pivotal penalty in the World Cup Final, missing the goal doesn't mean it's the end of the story for you. You get another go; that's the wonderful thing about life.

After I left Ratners, I had a couple of spectacular failures that didn't feel good at the time, but actually led me to where I am today.

The first was a factory outlet store I tried to set up in London. There was a fabulous old warehouse building in Tobacco Dock, near the Tower of London, that was going cheap because the owners had tried – and failed – to set it up as a shopping centre. (In hindsight, I was arrogant; that was the first red flag. Always learn from others' mistakes so you don't have to make your own.) A family from Kuwait had acquired the building, so I was working with them to turn it into a business.

The idea was to set up a factory outlet full of top designer brands like Ralph Lauren and Gucci at cut prices. In itself, this was a brilliant idea: the model was working well in other places, like the hugely successful Bicester Village, which at the time had just opened about an hour outside of London.

And I was perfect for the challenge: I've always liked to sell things at a discount, and I was keen to get the brands on board. What could go wrong with selling great products at 50 percent off? I got my friend Charles Saatchi to produce a fantastic brochure laying out the benefits to get the brands on board, and I started contacting companies.

It became clear pretty quickly that the location was wrong – it was too close to London. The key to making a factory outlet venture a success is finding a balance in terms of location: it needs to be in a 'dead zone' that's far enough away from the top city shopping areas but close enough to get to easily. Tobacco Dock was certainly a dead spot, but it was far from being in the middle of nowhere – you could get to Oxford Street in about half an hour on public transport. That's far too close for an outlet centre.

Needless to say the bottom fell out of the whole venture. Had we been working with a different location, it could have been a very different story. Location is so important: before this, I had decided against a location in Canary Wharf because at the time it was a real void spot in a horrible area. Now, of course, the whole area is a massive hit for retail, with millions of suits passing by every day and easy access with the Jubilee Line. Taking that location would have ended up being better than the health club I went on to establish. Isn't hindsight painful?

My failure didn't end there... I was on a roll!

Next up was my corker of a French failure. NatWest Ventures had taken over the largest jewellery company in France after it went into liquidation. They offered me a job running it, so I thought, ok, I'd better learn French.

I had a set of BBC CDs to help me learn, and a French woman used to come over to my house to teach me. I was doing quite well, I was picking up the language and feeling confident, and by the time I arrived in France to start my job, I felt ready.

And nobody understood a word I said.

I'm sure there was a bit of resistance mixed in there, and some people might have been pretending they couldn't understand me, but every day I was surrounded by confused faces – not a pleasant sight. They said I'd learned conversational French and I was talking too slowly. That's fine for ordering a croque monsieur and a coffee, but I couldn't chair a meeting or discuss a balance sheet. And I was just as confused – everyone was speaking so quickly, I couldn't keep up.

Just like with Tobacco Dock, I had made a basic error. The bank might have stuck me in that position, but the staff didn't want me – they wanted the management back in, the French leaders, not some Englishman who couldn't string a proper sentence together in their language. They didn't want me to succeed, and that provided the perfect conditions for failure.

Fail fast, fail often

I didn't hang about in either of those situations. When I knew the thing was a flop, when I knew it was going to fail, I didn't flog it to death, I gave it a dignified exit, brushed myself off and stood up again.

That's the key thing with failure: you've got to invite it, let it happen, accept it, learn from it and *get over it*.

When you reinvent yourself, you're going to be levelling up your (risk of) failure exponentially. You need to be willing to fail and get up again. That's the way to reinvent yourself – with anything, there's an element of try-fail-fix-repeat.

Reportedly, eight out of ten new ventures fail – certainly if you ignore red flags like I did. When you're setting up a new business, the odds are literally against you: you're four times more likely to fail than succeed. The likelihood of your venture being a success the first time is low. The likelihood of you succeeding the second time is low. The trick is to keep going and beat the odds – reach the fourth and fifth attempt and you're getting somewhere.

The people who really fail are the ones who give up trying. If whatever you're attempting flops the first time, that doesn't have to mean the end for you.

As a result of all this, failure has become some kind of holy grail in business – if you can survive failure, you'll be rewarded with success. That's the idea, at least. The reality is a lot less shiny than this. Failure is painful. It's embarrassing, maybe even humiliating – it certainly was for me at one point. It's frustrating and unfair, it can make you devastated, poor and livid.

I'm sharing this because you need to know the reality in order to get through it and come out the other side. I think failure has been glamourised so much over the years that it's become a glossy version of itself – something the high-fliers like Richard Branson do every day of the week, then share in articles about how great it is to fail and learn from your mistakes.

Let's get real: failure is going to hurt. We all know that, and it's precisely why we're so scared of it. Failure stops us from doing virtually everything because we're afraid of change and even more afraid of failing at change. That little voice making you question what you're doing: *what if you mess it up? What will people think? What will they say? You'll be a laughingstock. You'll lose all your money. No one will want to work with you ever again.*

That fear is strong, and it's understandable that it holds so many people back. But I really believe that you can handle it. Why? Because if you really want that reinvented version of yourself, you'll be willing to take the risk – to tackle the fear of failure – to reap the benefits.

If you think about it, it's a pretty straight trade-off. You need to risk failure in order to succeed, but you're afraid of failure so you don't want to try. Fear is the obstacle on your path. All you have to do is overcome it. Rob's got some great tips for doing this at the end of the chapter.

Don't just invite failure; plan for it

In business, you're constantly planning to fail. You need to think about the downside, the risk, the worst-case scenario, so you can build in mitigation strategies and business continuity plans. The bigger the business, the bigger the focus on failure.

In businesses, whenever I got knocked back, I would always try and come back into it. If I'm honest, this is in large part because of one of my less desirable attributes (but one a lot of entrepreneurs share): ego. I actually think ego is very important – it motivates you to succeed because you wouldn't want people to see you as a failure. That might seem like a funny way of approaching it, but for me, it's been one of the big reasons I don't fear failure – because it can't be possible.

Another part of my tendency to bounce back is what we might call FOMO these days – fear of missing out. It wasn't just an ego-fuelled refusal to fail that drove me, I was addicted to the thrill of business and didn't want to be left out. It's like the party you're not invited to, which absolutely must be the best party that's ever happened. In the aftermath of The Speech, I used to play a song called 'Let Me In' by R. E. M. as I sat and watched the world pass me by. It was my biggest fear – the fear of inaction.

That's something Tim Ferriss addresses in his 'fear-setting' exercise, which could help you overcome fear of failure (or any fear, for that matter). If you haven't seen it yet, I recommend you watch his TED talk on fear-setting. (More than 7 million people have watched it already, so if you're not one of them, why not go ahead and take 14 minutes to look it up and watch it. I can wait.) He has developed a three-step exercise, which I'll summarise here.

1. Define, prevent, repair. Make three columns on a page. In column one, write down all the worst things that could happen if you do the thing you fear. In column two, write down all the ways you could prevent those things from happening. In column three, write down how you could fix things or who you might ask for help if the worst happened.

2. Look for the benefits. What would be the upside of trying, or moving towards your goal, even if you don't make it all the way? Make sure you include lessons you'll learn from the process.

3. Consider the cost of inaction. Doing the thing is scary, because you fear failure. But what would happen if you didn't even try? If nothing changed? If you didn't take action? Write it down. Thinking about the potential pain of the status quo can help you overcome your fears of taking the step and putting yourself at risk of failing.

Knock-back leads to comeback

I want to end with a short but really important point. You are not your mistakes. We all go through setbacks, and they're good, they keep us grounded and on track. Try and think of someone who hasn't failed at some point. I bet you can't.

I learned this the slow way. After The Speech, I believed what they were saying about me in the press – the *Sunday Times* said I was unemployable – and I let myself become my mistake. It took me a long time to reverse that.

There's one person who's stuck in my head when I think about life-changing mistakes. When British politician Michael Gove was vying for Tory leadership and it came out that he had taken drugs at university, he was hauled through the press. He said on the Andrew Marr show, 'people should never be defined by the worst decisions they made.'

As a British person, I think the Americans have a lot to teach us about failure. There's a real comeback culture, and people are motivated to turn their mistakes into fortunes – or good stories, at the very least. It's much more common (and far less of a big deal) to be fired in the US, so I think people get more practice at bouncing back. We're much harsher about failure in the UK, and the culture around it is pretty unforgiving, right down to the shame of being sacked.

The thing to remember is that failing doesn't make you a failure. It doesn't define you. Look at it for what it is and move on.

Rob: Overcome your fear of failure

I might exude confidence and success (I'm writing this with a wink, in case you didn't read it that way) but I'm not immune to fear. Everyone fears failure on some level; it's totally natural, especially if you've got something big, important or meaningful to lose.

When I was a struggling artist, I had already 'failed' at being an architect, and I'd taken the apparently risky leap into an uncertain career – one I had zero experience in. (I was an excellent artist, I just sucked at selling it. Which is why my old art is all over the walls of my house rather than being copious amounts of cash in my bank right now.)

As I sat there painting, in the back of my mind was this repeating message: *why don't you get into property? Try property. Go to a networking event.* My Dad had been telling me to do this for years, and I guess his voice had wormed its way into my subconscious. I knew there was an opportunity for me there, but I was too scared of failing, of looking stupid, to take it. Sometimes the thing that's right in front of your face is still out of your reach.

Eventually, I overcame that fear and went to a networking event, met my business partner Mark homer, and the rest, as they say, is history. Fear is a real bastard. It has a great way of tricking you into feeling like it's insurmountable, but it isn't. In fact, you can harness it, control it and even use it to your advantage.

Psychologists have studied this for decades, and people have written books about it; I'll share some of the steps many of them have in common and some of my own.

(Re)define failure. There's a lot of talk out there about what success looks like, but what would failure look like? What would real failure look like compared to what you're worried about? Imagine you're starting a new business venture; you might be scared that you won't make it to five years. But actual failure might be having a significant and irreversible negative impact on people, creditors or the environment, for example. The upshot is, what you're worrying about isn't that bad and is also highly unlikely, so reset the bar – think about what failure actually is. One great example of this is Stephen King: when he was getting started as a writer, he would send stories and novels to publishers, and he would hang the rejection letters on a nail on his wall. He managed to collect a huge stack, and it was a major source of pride. He reframed failure: rejection wasn't failure; each rejection was taking him a step closer to an acceptance. Today, he's one of the most successful authors in history.

I have an Evernote folder called 'What they told me I couldn't', and each time someone trolls or hates on me, or tells me I can't do something, I put a little note in the folder. I collect these comments and use them as motivation to succeed. Even if I have to block, ignore or stay silent for the sake of my brand, I'm still going to damn well enjoy proving them wrong.

Feel the fear. Don't try to dampen it or hide it or ignore it, really sit with it. Fear is one of our most basic emotions; it's so ubiquitous in the animal world that it's something neuroscientists study in tiny worms. We all fear things, but how often do we *really feel* that fear instead of fixing it or running away from it? I think there's a fraternity of delusion where it's evangelised that you can completely get rid of fear. I do not believe this to be the case; fear is necessary for survival. Many times in your life you'll be very grateful you felt it. I believe fear mastery is about contextualising it, managing, controlling and then harnessing it, in that order. Letting yourself feel the fear might show you it's not as bad as you might expect. Face reality. See things for how they are. Swallow, hold your breath, have a word with yourself and look at your failure head on.

Visualise obstacles. You've imagined yourself failing – hitting the obstacle and then hitting the deck. Sit in that situation, feel what you're feeling. Now you can plan to make sure it doesn't happen. When you look at your obstacle, you can also see it as a challenge – one you want to overcome. Like a mountain you're excited to climb, a race you want to try and win. Fear of failure can be foggy, but when you focus on it, you'll start to see the obstacles outlined more clearly. Rejection by potential clients, hate on social media, an empty conference venue. These things are clear, concrete, and you can plan to prevent them from happening. It's wise to pre-empt future challenges as well as future goals and upsides, so you aren't setting yourself up for failure from the start.

Reframe your goals. We focus on success, and that's great, you get more of what you focus on. But life isn't as simple as success and failure. It's a paradox: success has negatives, and failure has positives. There are equal downsides in perceived upsides, and equal upsides in perceived downsides. One of the big positives failure brings is the opportunity for learning. You can maximise the upside of failure before it (potentially) happens by setting learning goals. What can you learn from the thing you want to do, even if you fail? It could be about how to set up (or wind down) a company or how to hire someone, how to create your best schedule or how to answer interview questions well. You earn or you learn. You win or you learn. Wisdom is in seeing the upside *at the time*, in the moment. Not afterwards, when it's easier to get the lesson you couldn't see when you were in it. There's always a lesson to be learned; if you make it a goal, you will never fail.

Learn from other people's failures. You're acing this step already by reading this book. Study people who have failed and come back (like Gerald and me) and see what you can take from their stories. Stand on the shoulders of giants. Learn your mistakes vicariously through others so you don't have to make them. Would you rather learn about bankruptcy by going bankrupt, or getting someone's past experience and warnings? Some lessons and experiences you do not have to have yourself to be successful.

This will do two things: it will expose you to failure without the pain, and it will teach you lessons from failure without you needing to fail. The more you're exposed to failure, even if it's someone else's, the more you'll put out your fear fire. It will become normal, less scary and you'll start to see failure as something you can handle. Your skin will thicken and your adaptability to harder and harder situations will grow like a muscle. You'll also be able to fail vicariously, which means you can learn from others' mistakes. (Take it from me, that's the best way to learn from mistakes.)

Be kind to yourself. This is something we forget, I think. The world is harsh enough as it is; be compassionate with yourself. Forgive yourself. Let yourself learn and carry on with your life, don't let those critical voices (whether they're external or right there inside your head) tell you to quit. It took me years to stop listening to those voices, I hope by reading about my experiences you won't waste as much time as I did.

Repeated failures

If at first you don't succeed, try, try, try again.

It's a simple premise, and we know it to be true. But it's not always easy to put yourself in the path of future failure while you're still recovering from past failure.

Here are some examples of people who succeeded because they failed, who tried time and time again, until they reached their goal.

Thomas Edison:

> *'I have gotten a lot of results!*
> *I know several thousand things that won't work.'*

A list like this wouldn't be complete without the legendary, persistent, world-changing repeated failure Thomas Edison. One of the most famous inventors in history, Edison is well known for inviting failure. In a 1921 interview in *American Magazine*, he said, 'We sometimes learn a lot from our failures if we have put into the effort the best thought and work we are capable of.'

Born in 1847, Edison was born in the Midwest and worked as a telegraph operator. At the age of 29, he set up his first laboratory in New Jersey, where he created many of his inventions.

He invented devices spanning a range of fields, including sound recording (the phonograph), mass communication (the carbon telephone transmitter, used until 1980), motion pictures (the motion picture camera), electric power distribution and, most famously, the electric light bulb. He was prolific, and it shows in the numbers: by the time he died in 1931, he had 1,093 US patents to his name.

But the process was far from smooth. Among the inventions that you won't have heard of were the electric pen, the talking doll and the automatic vote recorder. He made 1,000 attempts at the light bulb before he got it right, and his first version of the phonograph, using tin foil, was a failure – he didn't succeed until a decade later.

Edison thrived on failure; he saw each failed attempt as a step closer to success. He ultimately became America's greatest inventor.

Sir James Dyson:

> *'Enjoy failure and learn from it.*
> *You can never learn from success.'*

Considered by some to be the modern-day Edison, James Dyson has endured – and celebrated – his fair share of failure. Today, his name is synonymous with the bagless vacuum cleaner, as well as a range of other sleek, surprising functional products, from air jet hand dryers to bladeless cooling fans.

Dyson's success didn't come from nowhere. By 1970, as a student in his early 20s at the Royal College of Art in England, he helped design a watercraft called the Sea Truck, and then went on to create the ballbarrow – a wheelbarrow with a ball instead of a wheel – and a trolleyball, which launched boats. Apparently, he was a much bigger fan of balls than everyone else, because neither was a big hit.

Later that decade, Dyson decided to develop cyclonic separation, which he thought would work well in a vacuum without a bag. He spent five years working on his invention, partly supported by his wife's art teacher salary, and built prototype after prototype before he got it right. 'There were 5,126 failures,' he said to *Fast Company*. 'But I learned from each one. That's how I came up with a solution. So I don't mind failure.'

He didn't stop failing there, either. He launched a washing machine that flopped before coming up with the Dyson Airblade – now a staple in millions of public restrooms worldwide. After that came the Air Multiplier – a fan without external blades – and the Dyson Supersonic – a hairdryer.

By 2017, Dyson Ltd. employed 3,500 engineers and scientists and was the country's biggest investor in robotics and artificial intelligence research. Today, Dyson himself tops the Sunday Times Rich List 2020, as the richest person in Britain. His net worth is estimated to be £16.2 billion.

Arianna Huffington:

> *'Failure is not the opposite of success, it's part of success.'*

Today, Arianna Huffington is known as a news media mogul, having co-founded the eponymous *The Huffington Post* (now *HuffPo*). But she wasn't always successful in publishing her work.

Huffington moved to the US from Greece when she was 16, and she went on to earn a bachelor's degree in economics from Girton College, Cambridge, where she became the third female president of the Cambridge Union. She soon started writing books.

In the late 1970s, Huffington struggled to publish her second book, allegedly being rejected by 36 publishers before finding a match. Despite controversy around several of her books – for reasons ranging from anti-feminist sentiment to plagiarism – she has so far gone on to publish a total of 15 books.

Having married a Republican congressman in the 1980s, Huffington was a conservative commentator; in the late 1990s, her views and comments moved left on the political spectrum. She co-founded *HuffPo*, which is often described as liberal, in 2005, and the platform became an enormous success. Six years after its launch, Huffington became editor-in-chief when

HuffPo sold to AOL for $315 million. It hasn't only seen financial success: in 2012, HuffPo won a Pulitzer Prize, making it the first commercially run US digital media company with the accolade.

In 2016, Huffington left *HuffPo* to set up Thrive Global, where she is CEO. She also serves on the boards of several companies, including Uber. Her success has earned her a place on the Forbes Most Powerful Women list, among others.

As well as crediting failure as an important part of success, Huffington is a big proponent of sleep. In her most recent book, *The Sleep Revolution*, she shares the benefits of sleeping more – something she recommends we all do.

Jack Ma:

'If you don't give up, you still have a chance.
Giving up is the greatest failure.'

With an estimated market value of over $480 billion, Alibaba Group is a giant among multinational companies. But did you know it was founded by someone who was rejected for 30 different jobs?

Before learning about the internet, Jack Ma had not yet found his path to success. He failed a university entrance exam three times, and then applied for dozens of jobs, including with the police and with KFC, and he was rejected every time.

It wasn't until 1994 that things started to look up for Ma. He started his first company that year, Hangzhou Haibo Translation Agency, and started investigating the internet. His first foray into website creation was a site about China, which attracted some interest and gave Ma the inspiration for his next venture: ChinaPages.com. The site made 5 million Chinese yuan ($800,000) in three years.

After working briefly for an IT company, Ma founded Alibaba and set out to get investment, and won $25 million – twice. The company went public in 2014, raising a record $25 billion in its initial public offering (IPO) on the New York Stock Exchange.

In 2015, Ma founded a business school, Hupan University, in Hangzhou, China. In 2018, he announced he was stepping down from Alibaba to focus on philanthropy, through the Jack Ma Foundation. He has a long list of awards and honours, including a high ranking on the *Forbes* World's Most Powerful People and *Fortune* World's Greatest Leaders lists.

Vera Wang:

> *'I always see where I didn't do things the right way.'*

Vera Wang's wedding dresses have sparkled at thousands of weddings around the world, making her a top-tier designer. Had you asked her as a child what path she would take, her answer would have more likely included a pair of skates than a pair of scissors.

Wang started figure skating when she was eight, and she trained throughout high school. She competed nationally at the US Figure Skating Championships in 1968 and was on her way to becoming an athletic celebrity. But she failed to make the Olympics team. This was no doubt disappointing, but it also led to her career in design, which Wang calls a 'happy accident'.

She said in an interview with Oprah Winfrey: 'After my skating career was over, I had to find something else that I felt I had enough passion for, and fashion became that other passion for me.' Wang landed a job at *Vogue*, where she worked for two decades. When she was turned down for the editor-in-chief position, she left, and at the age of 40, she set up her own business as a designer.

Designing wedding dresses, especially expensive ones (the cheapest Vera Wang gown costs $2,900, and custom designs can go upwards of $25,000) requires an eye for mistakes, so they can be rectified. For Wang, that means accepting, seeing and dealing with failure on a daily basis. She has embraced this, and as a result, Vera Wang dresses are a household name in bridal couture. In 2018, she reportedly made $630 million, earning her a place on the Forbes list of America's Richest Self-Made Women that year.

CHAPTER 4
Set Goals and Visualise

Depression wasn't instant for me. You might think that my darkest hour was the day the headlines hit, or the day I got sacked. But it was more gradual than that, more like dark clouds gathering overhead before a storm. What precipitated my depression was the development of some really bad habits.

You know the happy ending already – I reinvented myself, twice in fact – but there was a period of nothingness, my Dark Ages, in between my downfall and my first reinvention.

After being sacked from leading Ratners, I gave up. I believed everything that was said about me in the press; as I mentioned in the last chapter, I believed my own publicity and thought I was unemployable. I accepted that my next job wouldn't be as high profile, but the city hacks were making jokes about me not being eligible to be a postman. At 43 years old, that was quite a blow to the ego.

I was broken by the press and I needed to give myself a boost; I started behaving in ridiculous ways. I was no longer a success in business, so I sought that thrill elsewhere. I'm full of gratitude and respect for Moira for putting up with me through all that; I certainly wouldn't have done.

It had to change, but that meant facing reality. What was I going to do? I'd lost everything and had come to believe that I couldn't do or be anything. I woke up every morning with no money, nothing to do and nowhere to go.

I did nothing for seven years.

And when I say nothing, I'm not exaggerating. I would sit in bed all day, reliving my mistakes, feeling sorry for myself, full of regret and anger.

I watched a lot of television (my specialist subject on Mastermind really ought to be 90s daytime TV). The highlight of my day was watching Countdown, for god's sake.

I shrank further and further into myself. I got to the stage that I was put on Seroxat – an antidepressant like Prozac. (Incidentally, in the 90s, the three most popular products in the UK were the iPod, Seroxat and Australian Chardonnay. That says something, doesn't it? I definitely wasn't the only person suffering with career and financial anxiety.)

The pills took the edge off the depression for a while, but that was the problem – they took the edge off everything else too. Those pills that were meant to stop me being depressed were taking me further away from the person I was; they took away the sharpness I needed to get back on my feet.

I didn't realise this at first, of course, and I slumped into my new routine of nothingness quite comfortably. Bad habits are sneaky, they just creep up on you. I liken bad habits to being in a room with a smell. If you're in that room for long enough, you get used to it. It becomes your normal, it's your world. You don't remember what it was like before the smell and because you're always in that room, you don't have any way of comparing it to the outside.

Being in that awful smelling room is like being in a job you hate, a marriage that's not working, a body you don't love but are used to. For me, that room was a life of failure with no comeback, of humiliation, broken spirit and, if I'm honest, laziness. It's so easy to lie in bed with the TV on. To berate yourself and tell yourself you're terrible. To do nothing to fix it, just in case it doesn't work.

When you're in that awful-smelling room, there are two ways of getting out of it: open a window or invite someone in who will tell you how much it stinks.

Well I did the latter, and my visitor – my saviour – was Moira.

Despite what I'd done to her at the beginning, she was so supportive of me. I lost everything we had, and she stuck with me. I behaved atrociously and she stuck with me. She had every reason to leave, but she didn't. I admire and respect her for that.

But she went a step further: in the depths of my depression, she came in from the fresh air and told me how much the room stank. She said, 'you can't go on like this' and she gave me a reason not to: she threatened to throw me out. Sometimes you need somebody to give you a kick up the backside, and that was mine.

Break your bad habits

You may not have a Moira ready to boot you in the bum, so you might have to engineer that spark to make you break your own habits.

I wish I'd pulled myself out of my bad habits faster; I wasted seven years being lazy, sitting in bed. Seven years. That's more than 2,500 days. Imagine what you could do with that amount of time. All I managed to do was get quite good at mental arithmetic and put on weight.

Bad habits get you into a rut, then you get comfortable. Then complacent. Before you know it, your reality is so ingrained you can't see it for what it is. If you've got bad habits (and I'm fairly sure you have at least one), you need to open the window, get some perspective, smell that bad smell in the room. So let's take a peek into that room.

What's the smell in your room?

Before you break your bad habits, you need to know what they are. It's good to take stock from time to time, to reflect on who you are and what you're doing and decide if things need to change. One good approach is to do an inventory of your habits and see what needs dusting.

The big stuff. What in your life do you know you need to change? Think about the bigger picture here, the significant stuff. Family, relationships, career, finance, home, mind, body, soul. Think about where you've fallen into a rut: maybe you're in a dead-end job, or you're living pay cheque to pay cheque, maybe you've outgrown your home, or you've lost your fitness. Write down a list of the big things. The trick here is to stay objective, look at this as an outsider. Try not to think about how you might change things, just look at your habits.

1. **The little stuff.** Now look at each of the items on your list in turn. What smaller, less visible habits are contributing to the rut? Let's take your job, for example. Do you feel stuck in that job because you don't have the time to look for other options? And is that because your schedule is too full or not optimised? Or your relationship, are you fighting a lot because you're both tired? Or because you've got into a habit of watching Netflix together instead of having actual conversations? Explore each thing as deeply as you want and try to spot patterns and habits that may not be working for you. Again, be objective here – some of those habits may be very dear to you, so avoid the urge to pretend they don't exist so you can protect them.

2. You should now have a list of habits that are not serving you – habits that are making your room smell. Look for patterns. Are there any crossovers – habits contributing to more than one rut? If so, these could be your best priorities for change. Here it may be useful to draw up three lists:

   i. Priority habits.

   ii. Habits you can change fast or easily.

   iii. Habits that require more work or time and are not priorities.

Be honest with yourself, however painful it is.

Congratulations, you've opened your window. Now I suggest you keep it open and air that room. Start making changes to your bad habits.

A word of advice: take this one step at a time and replace bad habits with good ones. If you try to overturn all your bad habits in one go, you are likely to fall straight off the wagon. Let's say you have a bunch of bad habits that you think keep you calm, including smoking, drinking coffee and eating biscuits. Objectively, we can all see that these things aren't working for you, but it's not advisable to stop them all cold turkey. If you want to quit smoking (and I highly recommend you do), quitting coffee and biscuits at the same time could dramatically lower your chances of success. Take it one step at a time: quit smoking, then switch coffee for tea, then stop dunking those biscuits and pick up an apple.

Set a goal to make your new habits stick

The thing about habits is that they're so automatic we don't realise we're doing them. The smell in the room builds up so slowly we don't notice it. By looking closely and objectively at your habits, you can identify the cue – the thing that makes you do them – and then redesign the thing you want to do following the cue.

Here's an example. Let's say you've noticed you're wasting too much time on social media, including as soon as you wake up. When your alarm goes off (the cue) you pick up your phone and start scrolling. You could replace the scrolling with something else, like writing down your first thoughts in a notebook, or putting on your running shoes as soon as you hear the alarm.

In *Atomic Habits*, James Clear shares his knowledge about habits, how to break bad ones and how to create good ones. It's a great read, and there's some really relevant advice for reinvention. In particular, he talks about the attributes of a habit that sticks – the things you can do to make sure you follow through with the change you want to make. Here are a few of the points I took from it:

Make the new behaviour (seem) easy. Scrolling through your Facebook feed is so easy, whatever you replace it with will have to seem easy too. There are two great ways to do this. The first is to reduce friction – literally make it easier for yourself to do it by adjusting your life and environment around it. If you want to start running, for example, you might get your running gear ready the night before. The second is to make it seem smaller. You can do this through what James Clear calls the two-minute rule: make the habit the first two minutes of the activity. Because two minutes isn't much, right? You can commit to that. The reason this works is that getting started is the hardest part – cross that threshold and you're sailing. In the case of running, make the habit be about getting dressed and stepping outside the front door, rather than focusing on the miles that will follow.

Carrot versus stick: rewards and punishments. The reason we build up bad habits is they're almost always pleasurable in some way. We get a dopamine hit on social media, we are comforted by bad food, we feel safe in the dead-end job. To make a new, better, habit work, you'll want to make it pleasurable somehow. That might mean treating yourself to a bubble bath at the end of the week if you completed seven days in a row or watching a movie at the end of the day if you stuck to your habit. You could also wind that pleasure into the habit itself: running while listening to an audiobook, for example. On the other side of the equation is punishment: give yourself a penalty for not sticking to the habit. Make it meaningful and significant enough to put you off failing. Like putting £20 in a jar if you miss a run.

Track the new habit. There's a clear link between measuring something and managing it, as many business leaders have noted in the past, and that really applies here. If you track your new habit somehow, like making a calendar you can physically cross the days off of, or listing the times you want to do your new thing and ticking each one off as you go, you'll be more motivated to get it done. I know people who went months without missing a single training session leading up to a marathon, whatever the weather and injuries they might have endured, just because they planned it and tracked their progress. Use whatever method you prefer but keep tabs on your progress. It will give you a sense of satisfaction that will keep you going.

Set goals for success

What I think might be even bigger than these things is having a compelling reason to do something. When I was in the depths of despair, I suddenly had the best reason in the world to get up and do something about my situation: I had to keep my wife. I was motivated, this goal meant the world to me.

To find real determination – something you'll need when you reinvent yourself – you need a goal. Whether it's in business, health, life or love, having a goal will give you a better chance of succeeding. And like we saw in the last chapter, by considering and even planning for failure, you can create the conditions to win.

Once you make up your mind to change something, when you have a really strong goal and you set out the steps to reach it – the habits you need to ditch and develop – you'll be determined. Motivated. Ready for action.

I've seen people in business who have been kidding themselves for years that they're not successful because of their competition or the internet or the weather or whatever million excuses they have. Then it suddenly dawns on them – the window opens – and they see what they've been doing wrong, they set a goal and they're laser focused on making it happen.

There are certain things that good goals have in common (Rob's going to address this next), and for now, I want to point out two kinds of goal: approach and avoidance.

An avoidance goal is designed to prevent something from happening. You don't want to put on weight, you don't want to get a divorce, you don't want to lose all your money. A lot of people take this angle throughout their lives, and sometimes it works. But I think it sets you up from a negative standpoint, and actually, it means you're constantly focusing on the thing you don't want to happen, rather than the thing you do want to happen.

An approach goal is something you are working towards, something you want to happen or achieve. You do want to get fit and lose weight, you do want to have a more fulfilling marriage, you do want to earn, save or invest a certain amount of money. You get more of what you focus on, and I always say it's better to focus on the positive.

Rob: visualise and plan

In chapter 2, we looked at embracing change, which I think is a huge part of reinvention. In my Six Phases of Change model, the first three phases (disruption, denial and resistance) are the chaos stages: the breaking up of the old normal, the status quo, how it was. The last three phases (acceptance, evaluation and implementation) are where embracing change happens. These represent the order(ing) process, finding the new normal, the more evolved, better way. Let's take a closer look.

Disruption: Challenging the status quo. Breaking up the 'old way'. What once was no longer is.

Denial: Fearing change; the delusion of progress. Here the fear and survival-based emotions, what-ifs and we-can'ts take over.

Resistance: Holding on tight to the old way. Justifying and defending how it's always been.

Acceptance: Realising that change is happening and surrendering to progress.

Evaluation: Finding solutions to challenges and change. This marks the start of productive assessment and emotions.

Implementation: Taking action on new decisions, strategies and tactics.

You need to move through these phases of change to be successful in any area of your life. I believe that a lot of your happiness is directly linked to your ability to embrace change, and it's also connected to setting goals and planning: if you can visualise change, you can learn to embrace it, and visualisation is vital part of goal setting and planning. If you do not fear change, then you're only really left with real, life-threatening fears, which are necessary for survival. You can even turn the fear of change into the excitement of opportunity and reinventing yourself. Understanding the six phases of change will help you move through them.

I want to focus on the denial phase for a moment. A lot of people fear change, and that fear makes them tighten their grip on life – they have a need to control, and they're always on edge that they might lose what they have. These are hallmarks of what's known as a scarcity mindset – believing that money or success or material things or happiness is limited and therefore trying to protect, control and hoard it. That does not make for a happy life. In fact, it can make you not appreciate what you have, and can even push away the very things you are trying hard to control. Like when you need to control someone so much due to a fear of abandonment that you end up pushing them away.

If you learn to embrace change instead, if you learn how to enjoy change, to see change as a thing of beauty, a thing of progress, of evolution, if you can constantly learn, if you start to find the unknown interesting, even exciting, if you stay curious about what's to come, then you're freer, happier and in a much better position to reinvent yourself. To me this is a simple formula worth repeating: all change has equal upside.

Look at the you from ten years ago. Look at how different you are today. Everything from the things you enjoy to the clothes you're wearing, maybe the person you're with or the place you're living. Sure, a lot will have stayed the same – you are you, after all – but look at how different you are. Look at your belly and your wrinkles, ha-ha. If I look back, I'm much calmer and more centred now than I was. I'm more able to control my emotions and less concerned about what people think about me (both to a point). In my 20s, I was fast and exciting, in my 30s I was disruptive… let's see what my 40s bring.

What I'm saying is that like it or not, life will change you and change you anyway – you are always in a process of reinvention, even if it's one that is gradual, that's due to the sands of time and not your own intention. If you can embrace that, embrace the concept of change and the reality of change, what's stopping you from making that process intentional? From letting go of the fear and anxiety and worry? Of setting goals and making change work for you?

- What if you changed your appearance every year?

- What if you moved to a new country every five years?

- What if you decided to reinvent your career every ten years?

Does that seem crazy?

Sit with those questions for a moment. Visualise the outcomes. What might your life look like with some more proactive change, some intentional reinvention, injected into it?

Here's why I think it's a good idea to consider this: it's smarter to reinvent yourself when you're successful rather than waiting for the failure, the emergency situation, the disaster, or in Gerald's case, The Speech. It's like bowing out at the top of your career in sport or like leaving the party at its peak instead of being the last person standing in a room of drunken idiots (me when I was 23).

Setting goals for reinvention

This kind of visualisation can give you some great insights into what you want. It works in a couple of different ways. Firstly, by imagining yourself in a situation, you can activate your intuition – get a gut feeling for whether it's 'right'. Secondly, studies have shown that mentally practising something, putting yourself in a situation, gives you a better outcome. This has been shown in weightlifters, chess players and mountaineers who practise in their minds before competing. Thirdly, you get more of what you focus on, so by visualising an outcome – your goal – you're more likely to focus on it and therefore work towards it.

This is where you turn your vision into a plan. Once you've got the need for change – the reason for your reinvention and, like Gerald talked about earlier in this chapter, the reason to break out of your rut (and stop being so frickin' lazy) – and you're no longer afraid of it, you can get started. First comes an intention and then some action in the form of a goal.

When you set a goal, you need to make it as specific as possible – you need to be able to understand it, feel it. Saying 'I want to lose weight' or 'I want to start a business' isn't going to get you very far. You'll just be flailing around wondering how the hell to get started. Instead, saying 'I want to lose 20 pounds by the end of the year by working out on Monday, Wednesday and Friday lunchtime and eating at least five portions of fruit and veg every day' is more likely to work. 'I want to set up a limited company offering plants, gardening tools and training online by the end of the year and achieve £1,000 profit by the third month' is more likely to work.

That's why the SMART goals system is so famous. Whatever goal you set, make it:

- Specific

- Measurable

- Achievable

- Realistic

- Time-bound

Try it out: choose a goal that's relevant for your reinvention – it could be the end goal or something on its path. How specific can you make it?

I thought about not talking about goals in this book, assuming that we all know about goals and SMART. But, let's be honest, *to know and not to do is not to know*. I think goals are like Karate Kid, the relic of the 1980s that's now coming back with a bang in the form of Cobra Kai. If you can see goals as a vital area of personal and professional development, you are dramatically swinging the odds in your favour.

I do visualisation for my personal goals, often during my walking meditations or last thing at night before I sleep. I read my goals document on Evernote and immerse myself in the goals – I imagine what it would feel like to achieve them, using all my senses. According to Dr. Joe Dispenza, the more emotion and energy you put into your goals, not just seeing yourself in the picture but feeling exactly how you will feel, the more likely your goals are to manifest.

Let's do a bit more visualisation now (you know you love it). Read your goal. Now imagine you've achieved it. Read this, then close your eyes and go through the steps:

1. Where are you? What is around you? What does it look like?

2. Who are you with? What is it like to be with them?

3. How do you feel emotionally – are you happy? Satisfied? Relieved? Excited?

4. Now engage your other senses: how does it feel, physically? How does it smell, taste, sound?

Visualisation can make your goals real in your mind. The more you know your goal, the more you will want it, the more motivation you'll have to pursue it and follow through with your plan.

Of course, it won't always go to plan, and you have to plan for that too. Every year I set a theme for my life. In 2019, it was having the biggest year ever. I had been inspired by Alexander McQueen's story to live a fulfilling and meaningful life, and to go for everything I wanted. So I did, and we had our biggest year ever. And that brought with it the biggest challenges we've ever faced. I'd planned for my biggest year ever, and all the upsides, but not the opposing and undeniable downsides. Throughout the year, I had this twinge – it had been 12 years since we made it through the last recession, and I had this sneaking suspicion that something was on the horizon.

It took all of a couple of months of 2020 to prove me right. I didn't see it coming, but there it was in all its glory: the spanner in the works, the COVID-19 pandemic (which of course I didn't predict). I was mentally prepared, though. Once I'd gone through the delusion stage, and as soon as I realised everything was going to lock down some weeks later, I was making plans every single morning for ten days straight: plan B, Plan C, plan D, plan E Plan F, Plan G and so on. I was up at 3am or 4am and working through to 9pm. Whatever it took. I knew this was serious and we needed to adjust our goals or face extinction like so many already have, with more to come for sure.

The great thing about goals is that they are imagined – they're not really real. You can change them if you need to, and sometimes you will need to. Because as you change, your goals change. For all the reasons your reinvention is necessary, you may need to reinvent that reinvention too.

Set your goal. Make it real. But keep it flexible. Embracing change will help you do this.

Playing it safe

Change is inevitable, especially in business. For those who don't embrace and ride it, the risk of becoming obsolete outweighs the risk of the new approach failing. The list of companies that played it safe and didn't survive is a long one, and each story brings its own lesson for your reinvention.

BlackBerry: from unavoidable to obsolete

Remember the 'CrackBerry', as aficionados called the device that was ubiquitous in the early 2000s? They were like miniature laptops: users could connect to the internet with the handheld phone, designed with a small screen above a full physical keyboard. That keyboard was beloved, but when the trend started moving away from clicking towards touchscreen, BlackBerry played it safe and stuck – some would say stubbornly – to its guns. In five years, BlackBerry went from market leader with sales of over 50 million units in 2011 to a straggler, selling just 4 million in 2016.

The iPhone still dominates the market today, but there was good news for BlackBerry in the end: sticking with their physical focus, the company went on to become experts in the internet of things, cyber security and crisis communications.

Lesson: don't be stubborn. If it's time to make a change, do it.

MySpace: from everyone's friend to MIA

We're a fickle bunch, social media users, and although there's a lot of talk about Facebook controlling our lives, it's our choices that determine the direction the platforms take. Unfortunately, MySpace didn't listen. When the site first launched, it was a sensation: people were sharing their music, friends and lives, and the platform was famed for launching stars' careers. It provided the basic blueprint for all the social networks we see today, and who can forget Tom. (Where is he now?)

But when MySpace was acquired by a bigger company that wasn't adept at following users' tastes, it was quickly overtaken by Facebook, which knew how to build a brand, give people what they want and spot the rising stars... and the rest is history.

Lesson: listen to the right people – including yourself.

Blockbuster: from DVD to disaster

If you can remember as far back as I can, you might recall heading to Blockbuster on a Friday night to rent a video or two (VHS, the dinosaurs that came before DVDs, those shiny discs that predate Netflix). It was always a relief when you found out the previous renter had rewound them before handing them in. Blockbuster was booming, and the continuous rise of Hollywood fuelled its success. The audio-visuals industry has always been notorious for making formats obsolete almost as fast as they were created, so when VHS was replaced by Laserdisc briefly (remember those massive things?) and DVDs and Blu-ray discs ultimately, Blockbuster kept up.

But they missed a beat when things went online, and it cost them the business. Now that more than 180 million people have a Netflix account, Blockbuster's physical stores are outdated (hundreds have closed already) and the company is struggling to keep up.

Lesson: keep your eye on the world around you.

Kodak: from inventor to victim

This company's name is synonymous with cameras: since the invention of the Brownie camera in 1900, it has been responsible for some major leaps forward in photography. The earliest colour photos were thanks to Kodachrome colour film, the first jumpy home movies thanks to Kodak's handheld video camera. But the company's run of inventions didn't carry it far enough into the digital age for Kodak to thrive. It left the company flailing, trying to find a niche – pharmaceutical and healthcare industry applications, document management, memory chips – but it's a shadow of its former self today, with a share price 96 percent less than it was in 1997.

The irony of this story is that Kodak was superseded by its own invention. In the 1970s, Kodak engineer Steve Sasson came up with an early digital camera – one that would have made them a market leader. But fear surfaced among senior executives, and, as Sasson told the *New York Times* years later, 'it was filmless photography, so management's reaction was, "that's cute – but don't tell anyone about it".'

Lesson: don't let fear get in the way of progress.

Toys "R" Us: from the spotlight to the shadows

Promising 'toys in their millions, all under one roof', Toys "R" Us was the mainstay of children's products in the 80s and 90s. The multinational had megastores around the world, squeezing independent stores and acquiring chains to keep it in the lead for years. But while the company had an eye on its bricks-and-mortar competitors, it wasn't so observant online. Then Amazon came along.

It's not the only bankruptcy-by-Amazon story out there (and Amazon, of course, wasn't the only cause of its decline), but it's a big one. By the time Toys "R" Us filed for bankruptcy in 2017, it had racked up $5 billion in long-term debt. The problem? People are no longer flocking to one-stop-shops, because they can find everything they need in one place: their smartphones. Toys "R" Us was another victim of changing consumer behaviour and a side swipe from an internet giant that got it right.

Lesson: stay open to new ways of doing things.

CHAPTER 5
Get Healthy

When you cycle a mile, you pump your legs up and down about 200 times. This activates your hamstrings and quadriceps in your legs, and it makes your heart beat faster to get blood to your muscles. Your blood is circulating faster, and you heat up, you sweat. You breathe harder, deeper. You start to feel the fog lift. It's glorious.

This is a revelation you might have had already, but in the late 90s, it was news to me – and it changed my life.

In my Dark Ages, I used to say to my friends, 'What do I do day after day? I was sacked, what should I do?' And everybody said, 'Take a breath, don't dive straight back in. Get your head right.' The problem was, I took that literally and let it go on for far too long.

After years in bed, and with the kick in the backside from Moira, I knew I had to get moving if I was going to achieve anything at all. So I got on a bike and started pedalling.

I started feeling better about myself. I was getting fitter, stronger. I was enjoying the endorphins. I gave up the antidepressant; cycling was helping me deal with anxiety and stress. It was turning bad days into good days. It wasn't making me any money (yet), but, importantly, it was helping me think clearly.

Exercise makes you think without the pressure. You get a certain kind of clarity you don't achieve in the board room, where there's masses of pressure on you to solve problems. When you're on the bike, or in the gym, or swimming, you air out your mind and think.

There's science behind this: aerobic exercise can make you grow new brain cells. Studies have shown that doing cardiovascular exercise – the things that get your blood pumping and make your breathing heavier, like running, cycling, hiking – can increase the number of brain cells you're growing, in a process called neurogenesis. And put simply, more brain cells means more connection, which means better thinking.

To this day, I cycle 25 miles in the morning when I'm not in the office – two hours of aerobic exercise to get my heart pumping and my brain working. I work my day around this: I cycle, then I have lunch, then I walk the dog and then walk to the gym, which is four miles away. I could drive or get the train to the gym, it's only a six-minute journey, but I don't. That four miles is the best moment of the day. I feel fantastic because I'm achieving something.

I listen to audiobooks while I'm walking – not business, but often historical fiction like the epic 26-part program on BBC Sounds, *Tuman Bay*. It's set in Egypt in the 12th Century, and it's all about how to deal with your enemies and competitors. It's my moment of zen in the day. I walk, I look around, I listen, I'm in the moment. Then I go to the gym, lift weights and walk stairs, and head home feeling great.

I'm convinced that a big part of the benefit comes from being outside, in nature. I'm lucky to live in a beautiful part of England, and my 25-mile route takes me down the Thames, through places like Henley and Marlowe. I go through forests, and I think being around trees is particularly good for your health – maybe it's the oxygen they're pumping out.

There's this thing called Peloton now, where people cycle together indoors. It might be right for some people, but I wouldn't do that in a million years. When I see people in the gym, pedalling on a bike looking at a television screen, I think no way, I'd rather be out in the fresh air.

That's so important, and I'm by no means the first person to say this. In Japan there's something called 'shinrin-yoku' – 'forest bathing'. It's not about exercise, but just being in nature. Breathing it in. Experiencing it with all our senses.

If you live in the countryside, this might seem odd. But looking at the bigger picture, you'll see why it's so significant: by 2050, two-thirds of the world's population is predicted to be living in cities. And a study carried out in 2001 showed that on average, Americans spent 92 percent of their time indoors. That's flabbergasting to me. Just imagine what it's like now, in the age of the smartphone.

As we noticed during the lockdown, being cooped up indoors, sitting on a chair and looking at a screen is bad for your back and bad for your waistline. It makes you feel sick, it makes you feel terrible. Even sitting in the garden, in the fresh air, can have a positive impact on your health. And certainly after the COVID-19 pandemic, I think we'll see an upwards trend in health, especially incorporating the outdoors.

I drive my wife mad because we always have to be outside, and not just when it's nice outside. If it's freezing cold, we go skiing. For me, the whole point about skiing is that you have fun on the slopes and then you stop for lunch, you sit on the mountain and take in the glorious view. Okay, it's freezing cold, but you've got all your gear on, so it's not that bad. I don't want to be tucked away inside. You feel good in the fresh air, and the scenery is better; I challenge anyone to tell me they'd rather stare at four walls than nature's beautiful trees, rivers, hills, beaches.

I'm 70 years old now, and there's nothing like a milestone birthday to remind you how important health is. I don't want to sound too cheesy, but by the time you get to this age, you really do appreciate the beauty of the great outdoors; what you don't appreciate are the polystyrene ceilings, the neon lights and the air conditioning units inside offices.

But you know that already. We all do. We know it's healthier to be outside than inside. We know staring at screens, watching people's perfectly curated lives scroll by, isn't good for us. We know that exercise helps. We know we'll live longer, better lives if we're physically and mentally healthy. It's an obvious thing, I already knew it in 1997. But people so often don't take advantage of it because it seems hard. It's easier to go for a beer than get on a bike. Except it isn't hard at all, it's just about switching the bad habit for a good one.

Whatever kind of reinvention you're considering, planning or already executing, you need to factor in your health. You need to be physically and mentally strong to make a change, to break habits, to succeed. Having a fitness routine on the days I'm not working – doing speeches, working on the business or mentoring – keeps me in good shape physically but also mentally.

Business keeps your brain alive

Mental health is a big concern – as big now as it was in the 90s, when antidepressants were so popular. We're all under pressure from all angles, and I don't think looking at phones the whole day is particularly helpful. In fact, I think it has the opposite effect of walking.

And as much as I love and advocate for walking and any kind of exercise, to me, physical exercise isn't half as enjoyable as exercising my brain.

Chess is a great form of mental exercise. I've always been a good chess player. Well, I've always played a lot of chess, anyway; I do tend to bend the rules if it suits me, when I'm playing against my computer (you can undo moves, and why not? It's not something you can do in business or in life, so I take advantage of this little loophole where I can).

Chess is also a lot like business. It's a complex, strategic game, and you're pitting your mind against some of the greatest brains in the world. I believe that business leaders have truly amazing brains – I don't think you'll find the best thinkers in sport or media or even politics; they're entrepreneurs, business owners, company directors. That's one of the big reasons I love business – pitting your brain against someone else's is fantastically enjoyable.

Unfortunately, I think many people are at risk of losing their mental fitness. There was a huge focus on fitness during the pandemic lockdown, with all sorts of online classes helping people stay fit. But were they using their brains? If you're just sitting around watching Netflix in between workouts, it's going to lose connections; if your alcohol intake has increased, your brain cell count has decreased.

Just because you've been sent home or isolated, it doesn't mean to say that you can't reinvent yourself, but you need to stay sharp. You need to avoid the brain fog I suffered from.

My top tips for brain exercise

- Learn a new language. Even if it's five minutes a day on Duolingo, opening your mind to a new language can give you a totally new framework for thinking, and it'll broaden your horizons. My favourite: French.

- If you want to watch TV, choose something you can learn from. There are some fantastic documentaries out there. My favourite: American Factory on Netflix.

- Listen to podcasts that will make you think. My favourite: *Great Lives* by BBC Radio 4.

- Listen to audiobooks that will inspire you. My favourite: *Pride and Prejudice* by Jane Austen.

- Read books – fiction, non-fiction, self-development – open your eyes, get your mind thinking. My favourite: this one! In case you want another suggestion: *Origins* by Lewis Dartnell.

- Play a challenging game. There's nothing like competition-fuelled thinking to get your brain whizzing. My favourite: chess and Scrabble.

Your physical fitness is important, but it's nothing without your brain, so you need to make room for brain training too. Your brain is what will help you navigate your reinvention – plan it, execute it, make it work.

I've always loved this aspect of reinvention – it's the exciting part of business. I take a really forensic approach to what I do in business, which engages my brain in a highly addictive way.

Rob: protect your mental health

Steve Jobs once said, 'the people who are crazy enough to think they can change the world are the ones who do.' I think there's a little bit of crazy in all of us who run businesses, and that's what makes it possible for us to be disruptive entrepreneurs. OK, maybe I should speak for myself here, as there is definitely a lot of crazy in me.

But being an entrepreneur can have serious implications for your mental health. According to a study by scientists at the University of San Francisco, about half of entrepreneurs have at least one form of mental health condition at some point, including addiction, ADHD and bipolar disorder. In fact, founders are ten times more likely to suffer from bipolar disorder than non-entrepreneurs. I've personally experienced workaholism (there, I said it!), loneliness, stress and distance from family and friends.

My dad has bipolar disorder, so I'm no stranger to this. He's doing ok now, thanks to the right balance of medication, which takes away the highs and the lows, but it's been bad in the past. And we're never far away from another episode, which can last years. In the early days, after his diagnosis, I used to think the hardest points were the lows, when he was in the depths of depression, and everything he saw was the worst it could look, the darkest, blackest picture of reality. But actually, the highs are really hard. In manic mode, everything's perfect, sparkly, happy, but that fantasy and delusion can be very, very destructive.

Our mental health has a direct effect on our behaviour, our actions, the decisions we make, and therefore on our lives and those of the people around us. When you're in any process of reinvention, it's really important that you're mentally strong, resilient, prepared. I think there are eight ways you can look after your mental health on your path to reinvention, and I'll outline them here.

1. Don't compare yourself to others.

I met one of my heroes a few years ago. I was nervous on my way to meet Arnold Schwarzenegger – he's been massively successful in the fitness world, the acting world and now the politics world – I had compared myself to him for a long time and he was very high up on a pedestal in my mind. But when we met, I had quite the reality check. At six feet two inches, he's an inch shorter than me, not quite the giant I'd pictured. He wasn't as confident as I'd imagined him, and he was older than I expected.

We compare ourselves to people all the time, and now that we're living on social media, there's nothing protecting us from the comparison curse. We show the world our best sides (literally, in the case of selfies), we put the highlights of our lives on display. We're collectively distorting our vision, and it's making us mentally unwell.

We tend to descend into comparison when we're feeling low, so we end up comparing our lowest selves to other people's highest selves. That's not fair on us, and it throws us into a negative spiral of emotions – jealousy, self-consciousness, anger, sadness, self-hatred... Those are not the feelings that lead to the most positive reinvention.

To prevent this from happening, this first step is simple: don't compare yourself to others. If you notice you're doing it, stop yourself and say, out loud if you can, 'there's no comparison.'

2. Remember you're doing well enough...

When you're on a path to something, whether that's in business or any other area of your life, you probably have a tendency to judge your progress harshly. You think you should be better, faster, more – you have unrealistic expectations of yourself. The negative feelings get stirred up in the gap between reality and expectation, and if you make that gap too big, you're going to risk damaging your mental health.

Now that doesn't mean you shouldn't have goals and ambitions but make them realistic and achievable – stretch them slightly, not so much that you're going to make yourself miserable. If you've never run a step in your life and you've just started with a couch to 5k running program, don't set yourself the goal of running a sub-three-hour marathon in two months; make it more realistic. If you plant a seed today, you're not going to be climbing a tree tomorrow.

One thing that can help here is to have interim goals on your journey. Breaking down a big goal into milestones along the way can help keep you on track and give you moments of celebration, which is also good for your mental health.

If you notice you're being harsh on yourself, take a minute to sit down and write a list of the things you have achieved, the things you can be proud of, to remind yourself you've got this.

3. … And you're good enough.

Imposter syndrome is rife among entrepreneurs, and you'll probably encounter it in some form during your process of reinvention. It can be strongest when you're trying something new. Imposter syndrome is the feeling that you're not worthy or capable or that you'll be called out as an imposter. That other people are more qualified, skilled and experienced than you. That you're not expert enough to do what you're attempting to do.

I call bullshit. I think we've all felt this a bit at some point, but you know what? If you're doing it, you're doing it! If you're not deliberately tricking or conning people, and you're doing something with good intentions, you have to appreciate your own worth, your own value, your importance as a person and in the role you're in.

Everyone has a purpose on this planet. Whether you're producing or consuming, creating or enjoying, working or leading, whether you're a banker or an artist, a lawyer or a musician, a doctor or a writer, an entrepreneur or an employee, a parent or a child, you hold your own unique position in this world, and it's valuable. You are valuable. You matter to people.

And you know what? We weren't all born geniuses or prodigies or maestros. I like to say every master was once a disaster – we all grew to where we are today.

4. Ask for help.

Loneliness is an epidemic of terrifying proportions today. Being lonely can have a significant impact on your health – studies have compared chronic loneliness to smoking 15 cigarettes a day or being an alcoholic. In one study, people with social connections were 50 percent more likely to be alive in their follow-up meeting than those who were isolated. Before the pandemic, an estimated 20 to 25 percent of people in the UK were lonely; who knows how bad it is now.

I think loneliness is a symptom that grows the higher up you get on the business ladder. The more responsibility you have, the fewer people you have around you – you're among friends when you're at base camp, but at the top of the mountain you're alone.

When I was having my biggest year ever in 2019, I had moments of deep loneliness – I was tackling problems and challenges on my own, because I felt like I had no one to turn to. It might have been our most successful year, but it was one of the most difficult years I've lived through personally.

I learned an important lesson: if you feel alone, under-appreciated, unrecognised or misunderstood – or all of them – you need to ask for help. If it seems like you've got no one to talk to, you have to build that network for yourself. Mentors, advisors, therapists – there are people beyond your own family, friends and colleagues who can support you. Getting a therapist has propelled me further in terms of my mental health and understanding of myself than 15 years of self-development study. So if you're feeling like you're facing life alone, go get some help.

5. Master your schedule to deal with the pressure of daily life.

If you're on the path to reinvention, it won't be your one and only focus in life. Let's say you're starting a new business. You'll be dealing with everything that entails, from coming up with a brand to hiring and firing; that's already pressure enough. Add to that the pressure you're feeling from other areas of life and you could tip over into overwhelm.

You want to be a good partner, friend, child, sibling. You want to be a good parent and spend time with your kids (because man, they grow up f***ing fast). You want to be physically healthy and exercise, you want to spend time playing the guitar or knitting or painting, you want to visit family and go on trips. Each of these things – the 'shoulds' in your life – put pressure on you. That pressure builds up until it's got nowhere to go, and it damages you.

There's a simple way to deal with this: compartmentalise your diary. It's cold, calculated and highly effective. We'll dive deeper in chapter 8, but the basic steps are: set the priorities in your life and work; block time in your calendar for these important things first; schedule everything else around this.

6. Be yourself, forget the judgement.

Are you really you when you're relating with the world? Or have you got some kind of mask on, or a barrier up? You might be hiding behind make-up or a beard, sarcasm or passive aggression, extroversion or shyness. I think we all have our go-to protection mechanisms, but if you've always got the wall up, no one is going to be able to see the real you.

This will affect your reinvention as well as your mental health. If you're not being yourself in your own life, your connections with people – whether they're personal or professional relationships – will suffer, and you will too. And if you're not yourself during your reinvention, you risk failing to reach your goal.

There's a lot of talk about vulnerability, and I think it's important. Often those masks we wear are to hide our vulnerabilities. But if you go out there warts and all, if you share your good times and bad times with the world, be honest and upfront and yourself, you'll see that what you get back in terms of support and love and connection is so much more meaningful, as it's aligned with you. The real you. Your true self and your values.

When I started sharing my therapy journey on social media, my content got some of the highest engagement I've ever seen. Why? People wanted the real me. They want the real you too.

7. Turn the trolls around.

Trolls and critics and haters, keyboard warriors, bullies. We've all seen it online, and it's nasty. But in our hyper-connected world, it's reality. People are anonymous, masked, hidden online, and the hate drips out of their fingers onto our screens. It can be heart-breaking, soul destroying, to be the victim of trolls online, and you may be putting yourself at greater risk when you reinvent yourself. But you don't have to let them harm your mental health or be obstacles on your journey.

I've done a lot of thinking and researching about this, and there are a few points to make here. Firstly, trolls, critics and haters are almost invariably strangers. They don't know you, and they're going to judge you regardless, so you might as well be yourself.

Secondly, if you read between the nasty words, they might be helping you somehow. Do they have a point? Is there a constructive message that could help you make good decisions? Maybe they're slamming your live video or product or service; is there a grain of truth you could apply to make an improvement? (I'm not saying they're right, but they may have a helpful point that's been bathed in bile because they're having a bad day.) Remember, there's a difference between a critic and a hater.

Lastly, don't react badly. Thank them for their comment if you have to; fight hate with love. There's a wonderful example of this: American comedian Sarah Silverman got some hate on Twitter a few years back and she responded with love, and it ended up being an incredible story. She had tweeted a Trump supporter in a bid to understand them better, and a guy called Jeremy tweeted a reply to her that said simply 'Cunt'. Instead of biting, she checked out his profile and started a caring conversation: 'I believe in you. I read ur timeline & I see what ur doing & your rage is thinly veiled pain. But u know that. I know this feeling. Ps My back Fucking sux too. See what happens when u choose love. I see it in you.' She completely turned the conversation around, and a friendship grew from that.

When you fight hate with hate, all you do is make the hate grow. Try a bit of love – you'll both feel better for it.

8. Read my book *I'm Worth More*.

Not to do a shameless plug, but it's only a tenner and times are hard, ha-ha. This book is full of strategies to promote mental health. It's probably my book that's done the most good in terms of how people feel about themselves, which of course emanates to all areas of your life. It could be a great support on your reinvention journey.

Arnie: Mr. Reinvention

'Work your ass off. There is no magic pill.'
– Arnold Schwarzenegger.

While my reinvention came after making the most disastrous speech in corporate history, this man's reinventions – plural – led to 'the speech that broke the internet'. That's where the quote above comes from, a speech Arnold Schwarzenegger made on stage with German motivational speaker Jürgen Höller, in which he revealed how he reinvented himself no less than three times.

If you want your reinvention to be easy, his speech will make for uncomfortable viewing. Here's the summary: set a goal, work hard and win.

Reinvention is woven into the fabric of Schwarzenegger's entire life. He was born in Austria in 1947, where his father had joined the Nazi Party and served for Germany in the Second World War. It can't have been an easy start in life, as the family reportedly struggled financially (Schwarzenegger remembers the excitement of the family buying a refrigerator when he was young).

It was also an abusive household, and he has recounted in interviews the physical abuse he received at the hands of his father. This provided the motivation for shaping his own life.

Becoming a bodybuilding champion

He was active as a child, and when his soccer coach took the team to train at a gym at age 13, he found his sport. His first competition came five years later, and he won the Junior Mr. Europe contest. But it came at a cost. He was doing a year of national service at the time, and he ended up in a military prison for going AWOL.

Training soon took Schwarzenegger to London, where he improved his English as well as lifting weights. He surrounded himself with supporters, mentors, coaches, and, crucially, he trained as hard as he could. He became the youngest person ever to earn the title of Mr. Universe, at just 20.

Chasing the American Dream

His next big move was across the Atlantic. Schwarzenegger arrived in the US with 'empty pockets, but full of dreams.' He was studying at college, working in construction and still managing to work out five hours a day, then taking acting classes in the evenings. It's just a matter of mathematics. 'There was not one single minute that I wasted,' he said.

In his famous inspirational speech, he explains how everyone can spend an hour a day improving themselves, regardless of how busy they think they are. That hour a day turns into 365 hours over the course of a year. What could you achieve in that time? He does the calculation: we sleep six hours a day (you need longer? 'Sleep faster,' he says), we work ten hours a day, and even with two hours of commuting that still leaves six hours every day. Where does that time go?

Getting into showbusiness

One of the enduring results of his bodybuilding in America is the 1977 docudrama (a part-dramatised documentary) *Pumping Iron*, in which he trains for, competes in and wins Mr. Olympia (which he did seven times in total throughout his career).

Early on in his attempts to grace the silver screen, Schwarzenegger had been turned down frequently because of his accent, which some were convinced would prevent him from having any kind of acting career in the States. But he persevered. He played first movie role, in *Hercules in New York* (1970), under the name Arnold Strong and his lines ended up being dubbed. Just six years later, he took home a Golden Globe for his work in *Stay Hungry*.

Pumping Iron followed, preceding a long and illustrious career as an action movie star. His action roles started with *Conan the Barbarian* in 1983 and continued, studded with legendary titles like *Terminator, Predator, Total Recall and Commando*. In 2019, he starred in the sixth *Terminator* movie, *Terminator: Dark Fate*, at the age of 72.

Leading in politics

Unlike many of his Hollywood co-stars, Schwarzenegger is a Republican. Having moved away from socialist Austria, he liked the sound of Nixon's capitalist America, and he declared himself a Republican in 1968.

Thirty-five years later, Schwarzenegger was elected Governor of California – or the Governator, as he was widely dubbed. He served two terms, and although his overall success in politics is hotly debated, he did make strides towards the state's climate goals. He also famously declined the $175,000 salary attached to his position.

Succeeding in business

Schwarzenegger was a millionaire long before he found success as an actor, thanks to a sharp business acumen. Running in parallel to his three very different careers in bodybuilding, acting and politics, his career as an entrepreneur spanned industries and decades.

He started out in the bricklaying business in 1968, using some of the profits a few years later to start a mail-order fitness business. He reinvested that profit into property, purchasing his first apartment building for $10,000. Other investments over the years included Planet Hollywood, a shopping mall in Ohio, fitness and movie production. His net worth is estimated at between $100 and $800 million.

Starting with a vision

When Schwarzenegger trained in the gym, people would ask him why he was smiling for hours on end while others around him looked miserable.

He puts it down to having a goal, working to achieve a vision. As he said in his speech, 'visualising a goal and going after it makes it fun… you've got to have a purpose.'

He puts his success down to this single-minded pursuit of a goal across the board, from bodybuilding to business. He also recognises, as the Stoic leader Marcus Aurelius did centuries before him, that life is all about overcoming obstacles. In a commencement speech he made on Instagram to the class of 2020, he talks about his personal obstacles, including emergency heart surgery in 2018, just four months before filming started on the sixth *Terminator* movie.

Whatever the world throws in our path, he believes those obstacles are there for us to overcome. *The obstacles that get in the way become the way.* Disaster can change what we do – we can lose our jobs, our homes, be forced to change direction and rethink things, but we can always stay strong inside. As he said in a commencement speech for the class of 2020, 'Ask yourself, who do you want to be? Not what, but who.'

Applying Arnie's wisdom to reinvention

Here are some lessons I've taken from Arnold Schwarzenegger that are useful for anyone on a path of reinvention.

Start with a vision.

You need a goal, but that alone won't work: you need to be able to imagine it, to know how it feels, tastes, sounds, smells. It has to seem so close you can touch it. When Schwarzenegger was recovering from heart surgery, he didn't just do his breathing and walking exercises every day; he visualised himself walking on to the set of *Terminator* to film the movie.

Forget plan B.

Controversially, he doesn't believe in having a backup plan, because all it does is distract you from pursuing your real goal – plan A. Every time you think about plan B, or put any work into it, you're taking precious energy away that you should be pouring into achieving your real goal. Plus, plan B is a safety net, and safety means complacency. So embrace the risk and pursue what you really want.

Declare little victories.

Your final goal can't be the only win. You have to construct the journey along the way, so it's made up of many small milestones, each of which is a celebration point. For Schwarzenegger, that was finishing a set of weightlifting when he was training for Mr. Universe, because each set took him closer to the win. After his recent surgery, that was celebrating taking 500 steps, eating a meal, lifting weights again. Every one of those milestones needs to be heading towards the main goal, and that main goal has to be in your mind all the time.

If you fail, get back up.

One thing that holds most people back from achieving their goals is their fear of failure. But, according to Schwarzenegger, winners don't just succeed; they are the people who fail and then get back up. Don't be afraid to fail, he says, 'go all out and give it everything you've got.'

In his 2020 commencement speech, Schwarzenegger recalled an exchange he had with his director on Terminator 6, Tim Miller. After two days of shooting an epic fight scene, Miller said to him, 'Arnold, you're a f***ing machine.' He replied, 'no, I'm just back.'

CHAPTER 6
Get Started

'Join the club as an early bird member and save £250 on the joining fee.' That was the promise my ad in the *Henley Standard* made when it hit doorsteps and newsstands in 1997. The thing is, there wasn't a club to join – I didn't even have the building yet.

The beginning of my health club adventure looked more like the middle from the outside. From the ad I'd placed, it looked like the club was all set up and ready to go; in reality, all I had was an idea. But I was convinced it was a winning one, and I went all in on making it happen.

As you read in chapter 5, I had discovered the importance of exercise and, along with the kick from Moira, that's what had pulled me out of my depression. I was cycling every day and realising more and more that everyone needed to get in on this miracle cure. Everyone would benefit from it. In fact, it would be the best product in the world – better than the iPod (not that the iPod had been released by then... we were still grumbling about the CDs skipping in our Discmans at that point).

I thought – no, I knew – that exercise would make people happy, and that it could make me rich.

Everybody's health and fitness mad these days, but not in 1997; health clubs certainly weren't as popular back then as they are now. Most people didn't even have a gym membership. I decided to change that.

On my cycle route, I used to pass an old book warehouse in Henley on Thames, near where I lived. It wasn't the best property I'd ever seen, but it had parking and that was pretty rare for the area. It was also huge, and nobody was using it – it was perfect to turn into a health club. The thing that really caught my attention was the outside space – there was room for a proper outdoor pool. The few clubs that were around then didn't have pools, so it would give me a competitive advantage.

The problem was that I didn't have any money. I was completely and totally skint. As you know, I had been a multimillionaire before my speech, and even though shares in Ratners went from £4.25 to 2 pence after The Speech, I still had to pay the tax over the shares based on what they had been worth. I had to sell my house and I was literally penniless.

It was the start of a new relationship with my bank manager at that point. I still needed a house, so he agreed to lend me £385,000 against the £375,000 value of the house so I could cover my overdraft. Things were quite different in 1992, of course; nowadays they punch numbers into a computer and it makes the decision for them. But back then, the bank manager had the power to decide. He'd known me for a long time and decided to take a risk.

By buying that house, I was starting from a position of negative equity. And after the failures I'd had in the meantime, I had no choice but to start my own company. The bank manager had faith in me, but he wasn't completely mad, so I needed a way to get the health club off the ground without any finance.

What I came up with was quite ingenious, even if I do say so myself.

I wanted to buy the old book warehouse and start a health club, but I had no money to invest. So I took the first step: I put the building into solicitors' hands, which anybody can do without any significant cost. After that, I figured I could tell people I planned to convert it into a health club.

Without the finance, that was never going to happen, so I reverse engineered it: I thought if I could get the members to sign up, I could convince a bank to lend me the money.

As I said, I had already spotted the opportunity to have an outdoor pool, and after doing a bit of research I found out that the pool is what really attracts people most, because it gives them the impression that fitness will be enjoyable. In reality, of course, if people want to lose weight and get fit it's lifting weights and using the cardio machines that really helps, not just floating about in a nice-looking pool. And the ironic thing is, in the end the pool is the thing they use the least.

But at this point, none of that mattered – all I wanted to do was entice people enough to set up a direct debit. So rather than advertising with rows of dumbbells and treadmills, I got a beautiful artist's impression done of the outdoor pool – exactly the sort of thing I knew would appeal to the people in Henley.

I made an advert using the picture, announcing we would be open in three months, waiving the joining fee (which was very generous of me, considering I hadn't even bought the place) and inviting people to sign up.

Sure enough, within three months, 850 people had signed up for the club before a single brick was laid. So when I went back to the banks, I had 850 direct debits for a business that didn't exist. It was rumoured at the time that the bank manager who put the money up in the end only did it because his wife was one of the people who had signed up, and he got some ribbing from his colleagues. Sometimes there's a bit of luck at play.

I have to say that the club never looked anything like the artist's impression, which was ridiculously over-the-top, with marble floors and all the trimmings – it was basically Buckingham Palace with fitness equipment. But when the doors opened, nobody remembered the details of that drawing, only how it made them feel.

I had come up with a smart way to start a club I knew was a winner, with no money and no risk to me. And I was in business.

Start somewhere

It took me a long time to remember this back then, but the thing that got me back up and running was that I just went for it. I did something. I got started.

People have all sorts of reasons for not taking the leap, and we've already looked at a few – fear, resistance to change, potential failure. In my case, there were loads of excuses I could have used not to take the plunge.

- People said I was mad – that was nothing new, but they weren't convinced about my health club idea, at a time when they weren't as popular.

- Going against my own rule – I always say you can't be guided by your own preferences when it comes to business, but I loved fitness.

- Lack of capital – I was skint, and what little I had needed to go towards keeping a roof over our heads; the banks wouldn't look at me twice.

But that's all they were – excuses. Of course I noticed them, and they might have even cost me some thinking time to get around them, but in the end, I pushed through and just did it anyway.

People always said I was mad, even back in the heady days sitting in my walnut-lined corner office at Ratners. So when health club mogul David Lloyd told me 'you're mad, you can't have an outdoor pool' I can't say I was surprised.

He might have been right in many ways – people prefer using indoor pools because they're warmer and more comfortable. But I was convinced that's not what would bring customers in; they want the fresh air and the freedom of an outdoor pool, even if the reality is it'll be freezing cold out there in February.

Guess what? The outdoor pool is what attracted people enough to join before it was even built. And you never know, maybe that bit of wisdom rubbed off on David Lloyd in the end: outdoor pools are one of the biggest selling points of many of his 116 health clubs around the world today. Now I'd never dream of saying I told you so, but...

It's (nearly) always the right time to start

Looking back, I can see I was in a sense lucky with timing: expanding the jewellery business in the 80s, starting the health club in the 90s, getting online in the 00s were all brilliantly timed ventures.

It's not that I have a natural feeling or intuition for this, it's more that I have a sense for market demand and as soon as I got some kind of encouragement (ignoring the people who said I was mad each time, of course), I knew it was the right time.

After that, I just pushed it very, very hard and took it to the limit. I always think if you hit on something good, thrash the daylights out of it, because there aren't many things that you hit at the right time. I discovered on those three occasions – jewellery, health club, online retail – that it was the right time, so I knew I was on safe ground. Then I milked it for everything it was worth.

The key is starting in the first place. Starting doesn't mean you need to finish, let's be clear about that. In fact, knowing when to quit is probably an even more important skill than knowing when to start. The truth is, you'll never know if something's a good idea or timed right if you don't start. You can have the world's best idea, but without execution it's useless.

To paraphrase Woody Allen, 80 percent of success is showing up. Or to quote Mark Twain, 'the secret to getting ahead is getting started.' You've got to be in it to win it. Start as you mean to go on. Start strong. Start NOW.

I could ramble on all day in clichés and quotes about starting, and there's a reason for that: it's really, really important. Getting started is the only way to do anything. In the end, you have to take a leap – that might be a tiny jump on the spot, or an enormous one across a deadly ravine – either way it's an active movement you make to set something rolling.

Starting something can be daunting, but you have to remember that risk isn't a bad word, and taking a risk isn't necessarily dangerous, negative or wrong. It's like Rob always says, 'if you don't risk anything, you risk everything.'

If you're scared, that's a good sign – it means you'll be aware of the risks you're taking. But ask yourself why you're scared. So often we think we're too old or too fat or too poor or not intelligent enough. But the people I see who are very successful often don't have all – or any – of the attributes you might expect them to have. The one thing they all have in common is that they're prepared to put their head above the parapet and go for it.

Take me as an example. I've got a massive number of failings – this book is full of them. I've made some spectacular mistakes, including the biggest mistake in corporate history. But overall, I've been successful and made a very good living by having the balls to be out there, confidence in myself, the willingness to give it a go.

My worst period was that seven years when I was lying in bed watching Countdown. I'm the same person now, so what's the difference? It's the fact that I'm no longer lying in bed; I'm out, talking to people, doing speeches, mentoring entrepreneurs, selling jewellery, *starting things*.

Use excitement to build confidence

I haven't always been this confident, believe it or not. If you'd asked me in the early 80s about where I'd take Ratners, I would never have believed I'd buy H. Samuel. That confidence built up over years of successes, which started small and grew over time.

I realised I loved starting things. It's thrilling – you get this buzz of excitement. It's the entrepreneur's drug of choice; the more people I mentor, the more I see this. And when you surround yourself with other people who thrive on that buzz, it multiplies until you can't get enough of it.

There's definitely an element of enjoying the risk – getting a kick out of making the gamble, taking the leap. But I think it's the promise of success, the hope, that is really enchanting.

The thing that switched in me when I got out of bed and started working to open the health club was remembering that excitement. I had been successful before, and even though I'd lost it all through stupidity, I felt that those same traits that had got me there in the first place could get me there again.

This wasn't an overnight thing, of course, but when I look back, the most exciting part of the health club adventure was the start. I had no money, no building, and everyone was telling me I couldn't do it (which was great motivation to prove them wrong). When it comes to satisfaction, there's nothing quite like building something from scratch, creating something out of nothing.

It's a sexy notion, the start. Big companies often try to replicate the energy and excitement of a startup, by setting up a new department or attempting to run an acquisition out on a limb, but they're hardly ever successful. It's because you can't replicate the start of something – the chaos, the life-and-death decisions, the excitement. This feeling, this culture, is unique to starting, and I think it's especially powerful when you're starting *again*.

I've experienced this startup buzz a few times in my life; going from an empty warehouse I didn't even own to a popular health club gave me an incredible sense of satisfaction. I did that, I created something from scratch. You can do that too, and it's not nearly as risky as you might think.

Start small and build up

You don't need to put your life on the line to get some startup excitement running through your veins. In fact, I think it's usually a bad strategy to throw thousands or even millions at something from the outset.

Bearing in mind that the odds are stacked against you (a fact that's thrown around in business but true), it's better not to go in all guns blazing, carrying a basket that contains all your eggs. If you do that and fail, you've lost everything.

Instead, you're far better off going in there and saying 'ok, if this fails, I haven't lost much, I'll get up, dust myself off and have another go.' After eight goes, you've got a very good chance of succeeding, if you use national statistics as a benchmark.

When people tell me they failed, my response is always 'good! You're not going to succeed with this venture the first time, and probably not the second time; get to the fifth or sixth time and things start looking up.' It's a journey, and you have to go through those failures. Just make sure they don't wipe you out.

If you're reading this, you've got the added advantage that it has never been easier to start a business. All you need is a phone, some time and the motivation to get off your arse. Here are four ways you can start without scaring yourself rigid.

1. Start while someone else is paying your bills.

Or at least explore your idea. It might be really tempting to throw your arms up and change everything – stick your middle finger up at your boss, sell your house and jump on the next plane to somewhere sunny to live your life as a digital nomad – but that's enormously risky. That doesn't mean you should moonlight or do anything unethical by taking business from your employer, but there's no harm in starting to explore your idea with the security of a monthly salary, especially if you're nervous about taking a leap.

We had a buyer at Ratners before I took over who was a great example of this (although he took it a few leaps too far!). He quietly opened a couple of shops while he was buying for Ratners and he would poach the deals we had with suppliers. He was being really cheeky in the end and he got sacked (not by me, I would have kept him on because he was so good at his job). He opened 26 shops in total, and the first thing I did when I took over was buy him out for £4 million.

He did something that a lot of people wouldn't dare to do – he was an entrepreneur who really didn't really understand the word fear. I think everyone can take a small element of that fearlessness to get started.

2. Study the competition.

You don't need to hire a market research company and carry out expensive surveys with enticing incentives to get the lay of the land. While I don't think it's wise to spend a fortune, you'd be foolish not to study the competition. It costs nothing to do that. When I was planning the health club, I went to 100 different gyms and clubs pretending to be a prospective customer. I went on tours, did trial days, and got all the information I could collect on their membership structure, facilities, benefits and customer base. All it cost me was my time.

3. Sell your product before you buy it.

A lot of people would start by spending a lot of money on development – they would run glitzy campaigns and make the fully functioning product or service, and basically sink their entire startup budget before they even got off the ground. But in the end, it doesn't add up to anything except a huge bill.

My acid test is this: sell the thing, see if people will pay for it. That might mean selling a minimum viable product, or a service or course that's starting in the future, or, like me, the promise of a club. Do this and you can still walk away with no risk whatsoever, but with a very good idea of how the market will respond. There's no downside.

4. Go it alone, for a while at least.

The first thing many people starting in business would do is take new offices, hire staff, invest in advertising, build up their overheads, spend loads of money and sink into a pool of debt. Result = failure. To me, this is madness. Not only does it jump the gun big time, but it means the entrepreneur is missing all the fun of the startup. You can do all that when the thing is successful; slow down and enjoy the ride. One of my favourite things about starting the health club was sitting in my portacabin on site and selling my heart out, all alone. I didn't need a lavish office or a secretary or a massive team of salespeople.

You can actually do a lot of things by blagging to make people think your business is further than it is. One brilliant example of this is Gü, the company that makes posh desserts. When they started selling their desserts, they hadn't actually made them yet – they were selling the idea of them by showing supermarket buyers the sexy packaging. The two owners didn't go out and set up a whole factory, they didn't hire teams of people. They went out on their own and sold their products directly, before they existed. That's the right way to do it.

Believe in your idea

A lot of this will be common sense to you if you have an entrepreneurial mindset. If that's the case, great, you're on your way to success already. If it's not, don't worry, these are all things that can be learned. It certainly wasn't all second nature to me when I started out. Business is as much a journey in personal development and the acquisition of skills as it is of profit and success.

I think having confidence in your convictions is really important. You have to believe in your idea, believe in the business you're building or the change you're making. You have to be able to sell whatever it is. And I don't just mean selling for money; this goes for anything out there in the world. You might be trying to set up a charity – you'll need to sell the cause. You might want to start a group on social media – you'll need to convince people to join.

Belief underpins this. It's what makes your story convincing and compelling. It's what makes your sales successful even before you have a product.

Look at almost any internet sensation and you'll see the 'start small' approach. A small Finnish game company started Angry Birds in 2003 and celebrated 1 billion downloads less than a decade later. Instagram started in 2010 as a team of four and within 18 months grew to 13 people and sold to Facebook for $1 billion. And Facebook itself is part of the dorm room pack – companies started out by students that turned into giant enterprises (Airbnb is another, and of course, Apple and Microsoft).

Facebook famously had a sign on the office wall declaring 'Done is better than perfect'. This reflects the idea that you just have to start – do something, get the thing moving. But it's also about believing in your ideas and accepting something less than perfection, because you know it's going to work in the end. Because if you don't believe in yourself, who else is going to?

Rob: Start now, get perfect later

Step 1: read my book *Start Now, Get Perfect Later.*

Step 2: follow all the strategies and tools.

Step 3: job done.

Only kidding (a bit... you should read the book, it's my most succinct and actionable book).

I'm a big fan of acronyms and abbreviations – if you read my stuff or listen to me talk, you'll hear all about KRAs and IGTs and GOYA and JFDI (I'll keep you guessing for now). They're all really important for reinvention, but I think the biggest one for getting started is JFDI.

Just. Fuckin'. Do. It.

The first step is as simple as that. You do it. You start. You do *something*. You ignore the compulsion to make whatever you're doing perfect before it sees the light of day (because, let's face it, it never will) and you get it out there. Start small. Test before you scale. Start now. Get perfect later.

Grant Cardone is great at this. In one of the interviews I did with him for *The Disruptive Entrepreneur Podcast*, he talked about releasing books with loads of typos being better than not releasing them at all. He writes them, publishes them, lets his readers point out the mistakes and corrects them in updated versions. *[I'm having palpitations – ed.]*

There comes a point with editing a book that you have to just publish the thing. You get to a point where you get diminishing returns on time, reading a whole book again to pick up a couple of typos. Those ten or 20 hours could have been invested elsewhere for a far greater return. I also love the idea of using crowdsourcing to spot spelling mistakes and get feedback on books; like my friend Grant, it's something I've done many times over the years. If you have any feedback on this book, or if you spot any typos, send them to rob@robmoore.com and I'll give you a gift in return.

There's a huge amount of wisdom in this, because what matters most is the content, not the spelling. What matters most is the speed, not the perfection. But if you're used to being a perfectionist, it might be hard for you to make the change. You may worry about being judged, criticised or ridiculed. You may fear making mistakes. I'm not saying 'Start now. Get perfect later' if you're flying planes with 500 passengers or performing open heart surgery (screw all the training, just give me the fuckin' knife, ha-ha), but in the real world, on the streets of business and entrepreneurship, it's the quick and the dead. Learn on the go, as you go, not before you go.

I hear people all the time saying things like 'this is my last chance,' and 'it's do or die'. It might seem this way inside your own head, but in reality, it's absolute rubbish. The only time something is do or die is when you're literally staring death in the face. (So if you're planning to reinvent yourself as a modern-day Evel Knievel, don't just jump over a bus on a motorbike; learn how to ride the thing first.) You will almost always get more chances; 99.9 percent of the time it's not 'do or die', 'last chance saloon' or 'shit or bust'. You don't have to risk everything. You can test.

Let's say you want to start a new business, or create a new kind of art, or make a new product. You could give yourself three, six or 12 months, re-evaluate and try again. It's ok to quit. I think there's way too much emphasis on quitting being bad. In fact, I think quitting is great: quitting the right things, the time drains, the bad decisions, the things that don't work for you is actually good. You need to know when to shut something down and – here's the key – NOT feel bad about it. Not let it stop you from trying something else.

Think about e-commerce. You need to find products that sell really well. You're unlikely to land on the perfect product first time, you'll probably need to test nine or ten before catching the trend and finding the thing people want. Often, you're working out what will not sell, and you want to work out the losers fast so you can move on to the winners.

This means inviting fast, frequent failure and even faster feedback and fixing. Channel your inner Dyson – do it all with your eyes open, by testing and adjusting.

How to test continuously

I think a testing mindset solves a lot of problems, including making you less susceptible to (fear of) risk. It makes you a lot braver and more courageous. It makes you enjoy your business or life more. It helps you discover new solutions while continually moving forward rather than being stuck in perfectionism or procrastination.

If you're facing something that you perceive to be or hard or risky or big and hairy and scary – and reinvention is very likely to tick that box – your body, mind, emotions are going to react and possibly dig their heels in and resist your change. All your memories of past situations that created emotions that hijacked you at the time are going to rush to the surface. You could be scared, anxious, worried, reticent, overwhelmed, confused, frustrated, paralysed.

If things are big and things are hard and it's all or nothing, do or die, you're setting yourself up for a panic attack at best and total failure at worst. Your mindset is a.) inaccurate and b.) setting you up for failure from the start.

How do you eat an elephant? It doesn't need to be that hard, even if it's a big thing. Because starting just means taking the first step of the marathon. The first bite of the elephant. Every single big thing you need to do is actually made up of lots of small things. Focus on the process of going through the small things, not the outcome of the big things.

When Mark and I bought our first house together (ha-ha, that sounds like we're a romantic little couple), we didn't have a 20-year plan to buy hundreds of properties and set up a series of businesses. We didn't have a contract and a heads of terms and an SLA. We simply agreed that we would just buy one property, split the profit 50-50 and see how it goes. Mark had security to protect his downside risk and capital. We had equal upside share, equal responsibility, and we were both open to testing working together. We didn't know if it would work, you rarely do, but we managed to test each other out in a low-risk environment.

That's a first step, one that's manageable and one we could jump into relatively easily without being crippled with fear and anxiety – or a million contractual points and details and future fears that would have put us off even starting. Most of these details and situations that ended up happening we could never have predicted anyway.

Now, 15 years later, we own, co-own and manage over 750 properties and tenants, soon to be 960 when our current developments are complete. We built it up slowly, step by step. We got started. We *just fuckin' did it*. Had I really thought deeply and tried to cover all variables of nearly 1,000 rental units, I would have retreated back into my hole and done nothing, for sure: too big, too scary.

I still use the *Start now. Get perfect* later approach in many areas of my life. New joint ventures, new launches, Facebook Supporter program and Stars feature offers, most social media posts. Let's be honest, we all used the *Start now. Get perfect later* approach in the bedroom, right? … Right?

The other bonus is that it's faster to work this way – you jump in at the shallow end and walk as far as you can before you start swimming, instead of learning to swim and then jumping in the deep end. If you do it that way round, you've missed the start of the race. Speed is a massive commodity right now. It's the quick and the dead. The gap between the quick and the slow is widening.

So I think a testing mentality is much better than an all-in or a do-or-die mentality. You can evolve over time, and you actually get better and better and better, for ever and ever. Here's how you can make the testing, *Start now. Get perfect later* mentality work for you.

1. Start.

You can't test something if you haven't started it yet, so suck it up and get going. Make the decision (remember, it doesn't have to be forever) and take the first step. That might be picking up the phone or sending an email, doing a Google search or opening your CV to update, getting in the car to look at a new place to live or downloading that 5K running app. *Just fuckin' do it.*

2. Set a goal for your first milestone.

Now you've got a bit of momentum, think about your minimum viable product (MVP) – what could you put out into the world that's on your path to your goal? If you're developing an actual product, it could be a mock-up of the packaging or a version made of cardboard. If you're planning to completely redecorate your house, it could be a mood board. If you want to start a new career it could be a list of vacancies or courses you could take.

3. Set KPIs.

It's good to set some KPIs at this point – markers you can measure your progress against. These could be anything but should be relevant to what you're trying to achieve. Think about things like survey responses, email subscriptions, people you've spoken to or interviewed, jobs or courses you've applied for (and the application itself could be the KPI, not necessarily landing the position!), or weight you want to lose.

4. Review.

Keep taking steps. When you reach your first milestone, review where you are. Look at your KPIs; have you reached them? Are things working for you? What could you adjust or update to help make your path smoother?

5. Tweak.

Adjust what you're doing based on step 3. This is important: do it without judgement. If you didn't reach your goal, you're not a failure. Just make a change, a small tweak, and continue. This is the beauty of the testing approach – you just keep adjusting until you reach the sweet spot.

6. Repeat.

Set more milestones with KPIs. Take more steps. Adjust what you're doing. Rinse and repeat. Eventually you'll reach your goal and, in some cases, that all-elusive perfection.

7. Scale

Once you have followed these steps, you have proof, confidence and experience, and you've repeated the process a few times, then you can scale. Scale big and scale with lower risk; scaling too slow or too fast is dangerous.

8. Know when to quit.

There's a bonus step here, because it's worth saying again. Quitting isn't necessarily a bad thing. If you're taking steps, reviewing, tweaking and repeating and it's feeling less and less right, if you can see it's not going to work or that you no longer want to do it, recognise when it's time to walk away.

What's the first step you can take right now? GOYA and JFDI. SNGPL LOL OMG WTAF.

Companies launched in recessions

'In these times of the "Great Recession", we shouldn't be trying to shift the benefits of wealth behind some curtain. We should be celebrating and encouraging people to make as much money as they can.'
– Mark Cuban

The world has seen many recessions in my lifetime, from the global energy crisis in the 1970s to the Coronavirus crisis that started in 2020. Recessions can be local, national or global, they can affect certain industries and pockets of society, or their effects can sweep across populations more widely.

One thing they all have in common is that they induce fear in people – often financial-centred worries. But, and this is an important thing to remember, fortunes are made in times of recession. The key is to do what nobody else is doing.

These companies were all started in various recessions and not only survived, but thrived.

Netflix (1997)

In 1997, we were watching the Asian markets with our fingers crossed that the financial crisis wouldn't spill over into a global one. Economies were unsteady everywhere, and very soon after, we witnessed the dramatic burst of the dotcom bubble.

It wasn't an easy time for a fledgling innovative company. But Netflix was born out of need: founder Reed Hastings reportedly came up with the idea for an online DVD rental service when he had to pay a $40 late fee to Blockbuster.

Despite providing the inspiration for the startup, Blockbuster refused to buy Netflix in the early 2000s and lived to regret that decision. Today, Netflix is worth $194 billion.

Microsoft (1975)

Markets were still quaking in the wake of the 1973 oil price shock, and the UK especially was experiencing a significant crash. GDP fell by 3.4 percent and unemployment skyrocketed to 9 percent – not a great prospect for a soon-to-be graduate.

Luckily, Bill Gates and Paul Allen had other plans. In April 1975, they launched computer software company Microsoft in Albuquerque, and they made $16,000 by the end of their first full year of trading – the equivalent of about $400,000 today.

At the age of 31, in 1987, Bill Gates became the world's youngest billionaire. Microsoft went on to develop Windows, Office and Outlook – some of the most widely used applications in modern computing. In 2020, Microsoft was worth more than $1 trillion.

Airbnb (2008)

Kicked off by the subprime mortgage crisis, the late 2000s saw an extensive global recession that left markets reeling for years. Right in the middle of it all appeared what would become one of the biggest hospitality businesses in history: Airbnb.

Joe Gebbia and Brian Chesky had been living on the breadline in San Francisco and looking for ways to make money (including through a hilarious cereal venture – it's worth googling if you don't know it). When they realised hotel rooms were in short supply for an upcoming design conference, they decided to rent out an airbed on their floor, and the idea for Airbnb was born.

The timing was great, because with the Great Recession about to kick off, people would be looking for low cost alternatives when traveling. Fast-forward a decade and the company was worth an estimated $35 billion (pre-Coronavirus).

General Motors (1908)

An earthquake kicked off a 'financial panic' that lasted from 1907 to 1910, having a big impact on business in the US. But right in the middle of the panic, entrepreneurs William Durant and Charles Stewart Mott decided to start a new holding company: General Motors. They started with Buick and the Oldsmobile and went on to acquire many other brands in the first year alone.

By 1962, General Motors accounted for more than half of all car sales in the US. In 2019, General Motors ranked 13th in the Fortune 500 rankings of US companies by revenue, bringing in over $137 billion.

Disney (1929)

Cultural businesses are vulnerable in times of recession, but that didn't stop the world's most iconic animation studio from starting out its journey to domination in the midst of arguably the biggest one in history: The Great Depression. Walt Disney Productions was born in a garage in 1929. Disney brothers Walt and Roy had burst onto the scene with their first animation *Steamboat Willie*, which starred Mickey Mouse and can be spotted at the start of today's Disney productions.

Following the establishment of the production company, they made the world's first feature-length animation: *Snow White and the Seven Dwarfs*. More and more animations followed, as did theme parks and a global brand that is now worth an estimated $130 billion.

CHAPTER 7
Sell Your Socks Off

1997 was a world-changing year: politics changed in the UK and the US, with Tony Blair and Bill Clinton taking the helm. We were surrounded by a flourishing media culture, with the world's most successful group (the Spice Girls), biggest grossing movie (*Titanic*) and the UK's greatest entertainment victory (Eurovision... I'm only slightly kidding here) lighting up the year. Tragedy struck too, with the murder of Gianni Versace and the untimely death of Princess Diana.

For me, it was a pivotal year: it was the year I got back in business. And do you know where I spent a lot of it? In a makeshift office in a portacabin on the health club site in Henley. I loved every minute.

When I was getting the health club off the ground, being on my knees certainly helped. That might sound a bit counterintuitive, but hear me out. When you have nothing, you also have nothing to lose. You have less to risk. You don't have as far to fall.

But you also appreciate things more – you notice the little things. Take my makeshift office for example. While the builders were working away converting the book warehouse into my stunning health club, complete with outdoor pool, I was sitting in a portacabin, showing people how it was going to look. All I could give them was the image I had in my mind, translated so beautifully by the artist for the ad I'd placed.

Put that image alongside where I'd been before: on an expensive chair in a 40-foot office on Stratton Street Mayfair, the most expensive part of London, decked out in antiques. Quite a contrast.

But the biggest contrast was happening in me: I felt happier and more alive in that portacabin than I ever did in my plush Mayfair office. I didn't have to pretend that I was somebody important. I had the buzz of creating a business from scratch. And I had the motivation to win, because the only way really was up.

Once the club opened, I didn't have to sit outside anymore (though a part of me missed it, and still does). But the slog wasn't over: to make the place a success, I had to keep selling memberships.

I really enjoyed getting stuck in with sales and marketing; everything we did was intended to go against the grain – we didn't want to be another David Lloyd. I would personally show people around the gym and talk to them about what they needed. We always had an offer on the go, with no joining fee if you signed up before a certain deadline. We never discounted the monthly payments; that was just good financial decision making.

It was the creative ads I loved the most. We were continually advertising in the local paper, doing some quite controversial and (I think) funny adverts. One said 'If you're fat and ugly, join our club. You'll still be ugly, but you won't be fat.' Another one bounced off of a chocolate bar ad that was running at the time (and I bet you'll sing this if you remember it): 'If you like a lot of chocolate on your biscuit, join our club.'

What really got us the attention, and ultimately the members, was the free publicity that stemmed from my notoriety. Ironically, it was the fact that I was known through The Speech that got us some very high-value PR when we launched. I took part in a BBC2 documentary called *Trouble at the Top* – an hour-long episode following me around as I launched the club.

In less than two years, I had a health club that was 2,700 members strong. I was in a great position – I had the only club like it in Henley, and it was turning out to be a big success. That's not a situation you'd see today; even small towns are likely to have more than one gym or health club.

I've always kept an eye on the competition, and while there was nothing locally, I did eventually find a second club about half an hour away in Beaconsfield. It had all the features I had looked for in the first location, and for all the same reasons it was set to be a sure-fire success.

Then, out of left field, came a conundrum (and not the nine-letter kind): someone offered me £3.9 million for the Henley club.

I had a decision to make.

On the face of it, this decision might seem easy: I was running a successful business and there was an opportunity to expand on that and multiply the success. I was enjoying myself – it was something different, and it still had the new-venture buzz – and after two years, I knew enough about the industry to make a good go of it.

But I didn't do that; I made the tough decision to sell. No matter how good the club might have turned out to be, getting a lump sum like that and carrying forward my huge losses from Ratners would mean paying no tax. I had been skint for seven years, and I couldn't resist that big juicy carrot. But it was more than that: it was a great price for the business, which had 2,700 members paying £48 per month. And here was the clincher: I knew I couldn't go on and on forever. It was time for something new.

In hindsight, which is almost always crystal clear, it was the right decision – I was right to cash out. I think the notion that you have to retire at the top of your game, leave the party while it's still swinging, quit while you're ahead, is spot on. I was at the top of my game in the health club business. I'd got in at the right time and I got out at the right time too. And although Beaconsfield gym now has 8,000 members (I still keep a finger on the pulse, of course), I have no regrets.

I still get a kick out of it when I think about that sale. I had invested £200 of my own cash in a newspaper ad, and within three years, I had walked away with almost £4 million. Not a bad return on investment.

Always be selling

One of the reasons that sale went through was the success built by the two years of membership sales that preceded it. Which started before I even had the building. None of that would have happened if I'd been quiet or timid about my idea or about the club.

I've always observed great salespeople and learned from them. Take cold calls for example. Some people get very annoyed when they receive a cold call, and they slam the phone down. I never slam down the phone – I respect somebody who's trying to sell, because that's what we're all doing the whole time, really. But a lot of people feel embarrassed, they think it's beneath them to sell.

Selling has always been a big part of my life. I learned my trade by going down to Petticoat Lane Market in the east end of London on a Sunday morning and listening to the stall owners literally screaming their offers to the customers.

I started off selling in the shop for Ratners, and nothing has changed since then, fundamentally. I was three feet behind the customer behind the counter, trying to sell them a watch or a ring, and I'm still doing the same thing today, in a different way.

The number one limiting factor I see in retail now is that people are too nice. They're too quiet, too gentlemanly. You have to shout if you want to cut through the noise.

At Ratners, we did that with posters and pop music. While the competition was trying to be demure and elegant, we were shouting our deals from the rooftops, and it showed in the numbers. At the time, everyone said what we were doing was abhorrent in the jewellery market. But the fact was that most companies were aiming at a different pocket of society – they were going for the older generation with the money, people who responded to the chandeliers and velvet paths laid out, to ringing the doorbell and handing over thousands of pounds on one-off purchases.

We wanted to appeal to the younger generation – the new money, the 16-to-24s with enough disposable income to walk through the doors again and again. By playing pop music and having no doors to open and salespeople not wearing suits, we made the stores approachable. The customers we wanted to sell to felt that they could come in (and afford to bother) – and they were right.

Now, of course, demographics have shifted and the high bar for first-time buyers, increased living expenses and a challenging job market have pushed the sweet spot back up to the older generation (effectively the very same people I was selling to back then; they must have great jewellery boxes).

This applies to any industry, any product, any idea: you have to be loud; people have to hear your message. That might look very different, depending on what you're selling, to whom and when, and you'll be able to figure that out with some detective work (keep reading). Whatever your situation, people will only buy what you're selling if they know about it. And that's where visibility comes in.

Put a spotlight on what you want to sell

Now remember, I was in the fortunate (or rather unfortunate, if you think about it) position of being very much in the public eye following The Speech. As far as the health club was concerned, that really did help: when I opened the club, everyone knew about it. Because everybody made fun of it. But it didn't matter that the publicity was for the wrong reason, it made the club visible, and that's all I needed to bring in members. I got the last laugh.

The most important thing in the health club business is people being aware that the clubs actually exist. It's difficult to sell the product blind, because they tend to all be pretty similar in terms of offering and cost (although I had the added bonus that there was no competition in Henley at the time).

Then you need to do the maths: only 8 percent of people in a town belong to a gym. At the time, I had 12 percent of the people in Henley, and I put that largely down to my notoriety. It turned a negative into a positive.

This is a well-known phenomenon: no press is bad press. PR gurus work on this premise every day. Look at Tesla for example, and its bulletproof windows. At the launch of the Tesla Cybertruck, a ghastly looking but technically dazzling creation, they staged a PR stunt and shot the windows, which were purported to be bulletproof. Of course, the bullets went straight through.

We were all talking about it after that, and it wasn't despite the unmitigated PR disaster – it was *because* of it. If it hadn't gone wrong, nobody would have known about that launch.

Knowing when to switch the spotlight on is a skill you can develop, and you won't always get it right. Go out too early and the flame might go out before you've had a chance to sell; leave it too late and the interest might have died, or worse, someone else might have jumped in there first. There are a few questions you can ask yourself to figure out when to make what you're selling visible.

1. Do you have something to show people? As we saw in the last chapter, that doesn't have to be the fully developed product or service or idea, but could you at least show a package, an artist's impression or a synopsis?

2. Do you know who you want to be visible to? I'm sure you've heard a lot about target audience, but it's discussed a lot because it's important. Who do you want to sell to (eventually)? The scattergun approach doesn't work, especially not these days, so trying to reach anyone and everyone will not be helpful to you. The more specific you can be about your target audience, the easier it will be to get their attention.

3. Do you want people to think, feel or do something at this point? You need to be ready to get a reaction from your audience. That might not be a sale, it could just be a positive feeling connected to your brand or your idea. If you don't need anything from your audience yet, it might not be time to get visible.

4. Is your product, service or idea protected? Think about copyright, intellectual property and ownership before throwing it out to the public.

The M-word

If we're talking sales, in most cases we're talking about revenue, profit, money. In my experience, it's uncomfortable for people at both ends of the process: at the beginning, they're reluctant to spend it, and at the end they're embarrassed to earn it.

I want to take a moment to address this now, because if this is you, it's time to get a grip on your money mindset.

On a side note, Rob has written a fantastic book on this topic, called *Money*, and I highly recommend you read it to get a comprehensive understanding of everything, from what money is and how it works to how to make loads of it.

Profit

The first thing I want to tell you is that it's ok to make money. Get that straight in your head before you start, otherwise you'll be setting yourself up for some pretty lousy numbers, and if you plan for your reinvention to be your new income, you'll be headed straight for failure.

Business is about maximising your profit, whether you're working for yourself or running a public company. Profit is not a dirty word; you have to make a profit. And you can only make a profit if you are completely focused on that target. Which means profit and money should be one of your goals.

In this age of purpose and passion in business, of working for a cause, or turning what you love into your career, it's easy to think making money comes in at a distant second, at best. And there's something healthy about that of course, whatever you do doesn't have to be solely focused on money. There has been plenty of research showing that beyond a certain point, more money does not equal more happiness.

I can vouch for that myself (I'll go into detail about the upsides in chapter 12): I'm happier now than I was running Ratners, and I'm earning less than I did back then. It's not about amassing wealth or making it all you think about, to the detriment of your other values. But you do have to embrace profit and money if you're going to make your (business) reinvention a viable one.

Capital

The second thing is that having no capital is not a decent excuse for not starting! I can't count the number of times I've heard people say, 'I can't change/do/start/try that because I've got no money.'

Rubbish.

You've just read my story. I had nothing, I went out there and sold my idea before I made it. The guys from Gü went out and sold their desserts with empty boxes.

This applies in all sorts of areas. You can pitch an idea, a concept, a summary. Let's take an example most people shy away from if they have no cash in the bank: property. You can get started in property, or any kind of investing, actually, without a penny of your own money.

The key here are the words 'your own'. There's a term people use in business and investing called OPM, or 'other people's money' – by packaging up deals, whether they're in property or something else, many people partner up with investors, high net worth individuals, and split the profit. It's a win-win: the investor gets a return on their money without putting in any effort, and you get a return on your effort without putting in any money.

One interesting thing to note here is it also matters where the money goes. My father always taught me that you shouldn't spend money where the customer doesn't see it – put all the investment upfront, make your offer shine. Marks & Spencer invested in better suit covers to increase the perceived quality of the products underneath without changing them at all.

(Of course, I didn't listen years ago – that's why at Ratners I had a lavish wood-panelled office the size of a football field, filled with antiques. It took a few more years for that particular penny to drop.)

Even when you're starting out on your reinvention in a small way, it's likely that you will need to spend a little bit of money. If it's a business, you might want a simple website, if it's a product you might develop packaging or a prototype, if it's an idea, you might invest time in developing it.

There are so many examples of huge successes that started out small, and I don't just mean the tech giants born in a suburban garage. You can find much more reachable examples than that. Go to any social media platform and you'll see content producers, influencers, experts who started out with time, a camera and something to say that could help (or at least entertain) other people.

It used to be expensive to get your brand, or indeed your face, onto a screen or into a newspaper – in the old days, it was a good £10,000 for a print ad and £500,000 for a television ad (I still remember everyone piling into the office to watch our advert for Ratners). But with the decentralisation of media and publishing, you can market yourself for free or for a small cost and get in front of your audience.

With any of this stuff, you could quite easily run into the thousands or even millions if you wanted to. Knowing where to draw the line on your initial outlay is a matter of calculating the risk.

Playing the odds

Another upside for you is that although risk is trendy, it isn't popular. Everyone wants to play it safe, and that could be leaving the field wide open for you. That general hesitancy is exactly why you should go for it. You won't make money, you won't win, by playing it safe.

Plus taking risk is the most exciting thing of all. Why else would people go into business?

Don't get me wrong, we've covered goal setting and visualisation for a reason, and they do have a very important place. But personally, I've always been more of the old-fashioned seat-of-the-pants type of person. I go with my gut feeling a lot of the time; my intuition is something I've honed over the decades. At times, that has been my downfall, but I've had a lot of things that have really come off by taking a punt.

I also believe in analysis paralysis: I think you can kill an idea or a project by spending too much time analysing it and going into detail at the wrong moment.

As we're seeing right now, business is never a safe bet. You've got to gamble, and as I've said, to me, that's the most exciting part of it – how unexpected how it's going to turn out. (Think about the converse: if you knew how everything was going to turn out, it wouldn't be very exciting.)

The biggest adrenaline rush I used to get when I was a kid was when I would go to the betting shop and put a bet on a horse (you could do that much younger back then). I got so much excitement out of it; I can understand how gamblers become addicted. You get a tremendous adrenaline rush from winning and losing.

I had a system I call horses for courses. I would look at the horse's form over its usual distance and compare it to the race I was planning to bet on. Let's say it was a horse that would usually race two and a half miles, and it had won the last three races. It seemed like a sure thing. But this race was three miles. I wouldn't place that bet, and here's why. The horse would be used to running two and a half miles, get exhausted and fall back over the last half mile.

I don't gamble on horses anymore, but I'm unashamedly gambling in the deals that I do and in business in general. The difference is that in business it's usually a calculated gamble – I play the odds. Even when I'm considering something that's a significant risk, if the odds are in my favour, I will take it.

I believe it's the same with people. Being good at one thing does not guarantee you'll be good at something else, so you take a gamble, a risk. People have niches, and often their excellence in one area will be accompanied by a shortcoming in another area.

When you reinvent yourself, you are taking a punt on *yourself* in some way. If you don't know whether you'll be good in that new area, that different niche, you're taking a chance. The risk could be high or low, you might be taking up a new hobby (low risk) or jacking in your job to start a company in a different country (high risk). I would treat this like any other gamble: play the odds.

With everything in life, I've always played the odds. That's how I function as an entrepreneur.

Take smoking as an example: I calculated the risk and then gave up smoking. I enjoyed smoking cigarettes, but the odds of me getting cancer were really high, so I gave up when I was 30. It just didn't make any sense to play those odds. You wouldn't take that sort of risk in business.

It works the other way too: the odds of you winning the lottery are ridiculous. I don't play the lottery because it's not worth playing those odds.

I could go on here, but I'm going to hand over to the man whose catchphrase says it all.

Rob: if you don't risk anything, you risk everything

I say that catchphrase at the end of every video I put out on social media, every podcast episode, it's at the end of every article I write – it's a mantra I live, breathe and believe. You can't be a 'Disruptive Entrepreneur' without handling risk.

I agree with what Gerald says about taking a risk: it's something you have to do in order to succeed, it's that simple. Too much risk and you are putting yourself, your company, your brand and your reputation at risk. Not enough risk and you can't move forward. Too much comfort and you get comfortable, lazy and you decay. Too much discomfort and you can break or lose it all. 'If you don't risk anything (or risk too much), you risk everything.'

Here are seven simple tips on managing risk that will help take more consistent action, appeasing your fears, doubts, overwhelm, procrastination and 'what ifs'.

1. 'What if' is a useful thought; it stops you being reckless (just don't let it rule you).

If you never thought 'what if', you'd make really dangerous decisions and likely kill yourself, even if only financially or vocationally. So don't deny your 'what ifs', just manage them. See how they serve you. See them as feedback that you are growing, learning, aware. Then contextualise those 'what ifs'…

2. What if it *does* work?

It's wise to maintain balance and perspective. If you're asking yourself 'what if it doesn't work?' then you should ask yourself 'but what if it does work?' If you're asking yourself 'what if I fail?' then you should also ask yourself 'but what if I succeed?' Extreme emotions are dangerous for progress, so in any new or unknown venture, like starting your own business and quitting your job, for example, look at:

a. Worst case

Worst case you might have to go back to a job. Or worse, you might have to take a 20 percent pay cut. Or totally worst case, you might have to start again from scratch. You may be humbled or embarrassed, but you're not likely to die. At least you tried to answer the calling, and now you have more clarity on what you should be doing. It's better to regret something you've done than something you haven't, although you probably won't regret most things you try, because at least you'll know, even if they didn't go your way.

b. Likely case

You'll probably make some mistakes. It may take longer than you thought or be a struggle at times. But if you keep going, you'll get better, and in time you'll get good. You earn or you learn, you win or you learn, you keep going and you keep growing.

c. Best case

Who knows? You could gain freedom, choice and profit. You could make millions and make a difference. You could be a wild success and leave a vast and lasting legacy. Who knows? Well, you'll never know unless you try.

3. There's only one way to know: try. *Test*.

See your journey not as an all-or-nothing, black-or-white equation, but as a continual test or series of very small tests and tweaks. Because that's how it is in reality. No one ever has all their ducks in a row. You have to start with the first duck. Reality is nearly always different from what you think, so you have to test to see how it forms itself. This helps chunk down and reduce the apparent scale of the new venture or problem. Eat the elephant one bite at a time. If what you do works, repeat. If it fails, tweak. Then repeat.

4. Create a plan. Chunk it down.

You'd run a marathon one stride at a time, and that's how it is with your new venture or scary situation. Small, consistent steps are not hard, they're just new. Big goals broken down are not overwhelming. Set your goal in the future, work back to today, break down the steps and metrics required to get there, and do them daily. By the yard it's hard, buy the inch it's a cinch. (RIP Jim Rohn and Zig Ziglar, who've given me many great motivational quotes along the journey.)

5. Get a coach or mentor

Who is the easiest person to lie to? You've got it: yourself. You'll justify anything to protect your self-worth and self-interest. You created your problems, and as such, it's hard for you to solve those problems with the same level of thinking that created them. You need perspective. Balance. An experienced, outsider's view. So get out of your own way and find a coach or mentor who's been there and done it. They have blazed the trail. They have endured the struggle. What you find hard now, they find easy. They can navigate you through the midfield. It's the shortest route to the most lasting success.

6. Create accountability

As you're the easiest person to lie to and might let yourself off the hook, you need external accountability. You could test putting your goals out on social media and telling everyone you know, so that there's pain attached to not living up to your proclamations. You could set up competitions with friends, competitors or even foes, as an energiser and commitment to your actions. You could set challenges and rewards for milestone achievements towards your ultimate goal. You could get a coach. You could make a bet with someone you'd hate to lose to. You could pay or pledge money to charities, or even to donate to competitors if you miss your targets. Some of these approaches will work for you better than others – try them out.

7. Ninety-nine percent of the things you worry about never happen, so...

GOYA and JFDI.

What have you got to lose other than everything? What if you never try? Who will you not become? What will you not achieve?

Risk-taker Richard Branson

One of the greatest sell-it-before-you-buy-it stories comes from the creation of Virgin Atlantic. Richard Branson, who was a 32-year-old entrepreneur in the music business at the time, was waiting for a flight from Costa Rica to the British Virgin Islands to see his girlfriend when the flight was cancelled. He didn't want to be away for another night, so he found a chalkboard and wrote an advert: 'Virgin Airways, $39 a ticket'.

He didn't own a plane, or an airline company, he had no idea how the industry worked. But he sold out seats on a flight he then chartered, and he was in his girlfriend's arms by that same evening.

As we all know, this opportunity-grabbing behaviour is something of a hallmark for Branson, and it started long before that first Virgin flight.

He started off by trying (and failing) to sell Christmas trees and then budgies, before launching a magazine called *Student* in 1966 to campaign against the Vietnam War that was raging at the time. This was the first application of a philosophy that would drive his businesses for decades to come.

Student magazine soon gave him a business opportunity. He took out an advert in it for discounted records, which would end up becoming Virgin Records – a label that would sign Mike Oldfield of *Tubular Bells* fame, the Sex Pistols and the Rolling Stones.

His LinkedIn profile reads 'Otherwise known as Dr Yes!' – he has a zest for life that translates into business and makes him take bigger risks than most others would. He has launched more than 400 companies under the Virgin brand, selling everything from wedding gowns to condoms, airlines to financial services.

He once said: 'If you spot an opportunity and are really excited by it, throw yourself into it with everything you've got.' This is reflected famously in his motto: 'screw it, let's do it', which became the title of his book that reveals his most valuable lessons in life.

Branson's world record attempts

He's not just a risk-taker in business; Branson sets himself big personal goals too.

- 1985: fastest Atlantic Ocean crossing. Capsized in the 'Virgin Atlantic Challenger' and was rescued by helicopter.

- 1986: fastest Atlantic Ocean crossing. Beat the record by two hours in the 'Virgin Atlantic Challenger II'.

- 1987: Atlantic crossing in a hot air balloon. Crossed in the 'Virgin Atlantic Flyer'.

- 1991: Pacific crossing in a hot air balloon. Broke the record with a speed of 394 km/h.

- 2004: fastest English Channel crossing in an amphibious vehicle. Crossed in 1 hour 40 minutes and 6 seconds.

Branson is a legendary risk taker, and it's his ability to roll with the punches and move on from failure that really sets him apart. 'If you don't succeed at first, there's no need for the F word (Failure). Pick yourself up and try, try again.'

He's not short of a failure or two to use as examples. Virgin Cars, Virgin Vodka and Virgin Brides all failed to launch the brand in new sectors. Perhaps the most public failure was Virgin Cola: in the early 1990s, quality wasn't enough to take on the goliaths of the international soft drinks industry. But he's certainly not one to shy away from failure. 'Do not be embarrassed by your failures, learn from them and start again,' he said.

His thoughts on success? It comes down to the idea itself. 'Building a business is not rocket science, it's about having a great idea and seeing it through with integrity.'

CHAPTER 8
Do the Unpopular Thing

'You've got to go back into the jewellery business.' Jurek Piasecki, who was the Chairman of Goldsmiths Jewellers, was sitting in the restaurant at my club when I was doing the rounds to say goodbye to everyone. He was – is – a friend of mine; I didn't have many friends among my competitors, but he was one of them.

'I can't do that, my name stinks in the jewellery business,' I said.

'I know…'

'Well, you don't have to agree with me so readily.'

We both knew it though. After The Speech, my reputation had been dragged through the mud, and my name went along with it. I wasn't about to walk into a six-figure job managing a jewellery chain. But Jurek had a different view of it.

'That's why you'll succeed,' he said.

It took me aback at first, what was he talking about? I'd effectively buried myself in the industry, how could that possibly give me an advantage? Here's how, he said: the internet. The internet was still relatively fledgling back then, and jewellery was still a bricks-and-mortar business. Online was all about marketing and publicity, which he pointed out that I would get – even if it was bad publicity.

'I've tried it and failed,' he said, 'but you'll succeed because it's all to do with attention.'

I went on with my goodbyes, bidding farewell to the people I had worked with throughout my reinvention. It wasn't easy to walk away from such a positive time in my life, but the weight of financial worry had been lifted, and I knew it was the right move. I was also enjoying the tingle that comes with the seed of a new idea.

When he first said it, I didn't even entertain the thought of going back into jewellery. But as I walked among my staff, smiled at the club members and looked at what had only recently been completely unfamiliar terrain for me, I realised the value of knowledge. Familiarity. Expertise. I had become an expert in running a health club, but I still had decades of expertise in jewellery. I looked around at people's necklaces and rings and watches and remembered how much I still knew.

Could I really do this? Go back to the industry that put me in bed for seven years?

That tingle of excitement started bouncing around with a flutter of fear. It was the turn of the century, when hardly any money was being spent online, and whatever money was being made was business to business. I'd be mad to try and sell direct to customers on the internet.

Bingo.

It was unpopular, unsexy, uncomfortable and inadvisable. That made it even more interesting to me; the more people tell me I'm mad, the more I know it's the right thing to do.

I knew hardly anything about online retail back then – nobody did, really – so jumping in feet-first was risky. But I knew it wasn't going to bankrupt me. Just like with the gym, I found a way to start small, set up the company without investing and risking everything.

In jewellery retail, overheads are very high – rents, security, lighting, staff to serve customers directly and so on. The thing that attracted me to the internet at that time was the ability to get a product to my customer with very low overheads, so I could undercut the competition. I think in general, people would rather go into a shop than buy online, but online you can find products that are much cheaper.

By 2003, Gerald Online was up and running. The fact that online retail wasn't popular meant the timing was perfect: there was very little competition on the internet. Specifically, it meant I could buy pay-per-click advertising at a very low cost, so the website quickly ranked high on all the top search terms.

For a brand-new e-commerce company, that was key: I needed people to be able to find the site easily without knowing the company or domain name. Major stores that dominate the e-commerce market today, like Amazon, Etsy and Ali Express, don't need to spend a lot of money on marketing (proportionally), as people go to them directly, either through a browser or an app. But in the case of the website of a jewellery company that doesn't have shops, getting traffic meant – and still means – directing people to your site, including through Google Ads.

Back then, I could sell an eternity ring by investing 3 percent in marketing – pay-per-click advertising was £10 for an eternity ring. That meant the margins were still good. This is no longer an attraction; today, that same advertising would run to £200, making it difficult to profit from selling the ring. If I had started Gerald Online today, the marketing costs would have been prohibitive, going against my initial aim to keep setup costs low.

The change wasn't instant of course; the marketing costs were slowly driven up over time, and we adjusted the business accordingly. One thing we ended up doing was taking a step back in the chain and supplying other companies that sold at low margin to customers. I set up partnerships with manufacturers in India and we were successful in supplying jewellery retailers.

Just like with the health club, the timing of Gerald Online was a big factor in the company's success. Gerald Online was among the early adopters, and the opportunity that afforded in combination with my very public profile was hugely beneficial.

Resist jumping on the bandwagon

Once Jurek had planted the seed, I knew it was an idea worth nurturing. This is one thing I think sets entrepreneurs apart: if I had listened to the advice being thrown around at the time, I wouldn't have gone anywhere near it. But I'm not one for doing the trendy thing.

A lot of people who are looking to reinvent themselves will look around at what's fashionable, what's hot right now, and they'll jump on the bandwagon. Of course, this can work if you're fast enough or find the right niche within the trend. But if all you do is jump on it and replicate what everyone else is doing, you're likely to fall – hard.

There have always been people who follow the trend, but it has become ubiquitous in business recently. I think it's a product of modern society.

Firstly, today it's easier than ever to start a business and call yourself an entrepreneur. That has led to cookie-cutter style companies popping up all over the place, promising similar things to similar people in similar ways. It starts with one or two companies doing really well (and often starting in a new and disruptive way), then more and more follow. They're catching onto a trend rather than thinking for themselves.

The more people do it, the lower the entry threshold becomes. Gurus and coaches start popping up and promising to get you a six-figure business rolling in a matter of months. But the bigger the trend gets, the thinner the slice of the action everyone gets.

It's also to do with fear of missing out – FOMO. If you look at the phrase 'jumping on the bandwagon', it comes from old-fashioned vehicles used in floats: a band would be playing, and people would be invited to 'jump on' and enjoy the music. In psychology, the bandwagon effect describes the behaviour of jumping on a trend or movement, often ignoring one's own beliefs.

Psychologically, this behaviour makes sense: the herd mentality means we 'fit in' with others, putting us in a safer social position. But it also reaches an unhealthy level in the form of FOMO: we see others getting all the good stuff, and we want some too. And because we're acutely aware of the speed with which the world changes, we have to do it now.

My solution to this isn't easy, but it has done me well over the years.

Do the unpopular thing.

This requires more effort, more thought and more risk than jumping on the bandwagon, but it will give you more return on your investment in the long term, not just in financial terms but also in satisfaction.

I think just joining in with everybody else in a new venture is the worst kind of herd mentality. It's sheep seeking safety – it's born out of fear of failure and change. When you're looking at reinvention, especially in the business sense, you need to be ready to take a risk. The successful entrepreneur is the person who not only takes the risk but seeks it out.

Of course it's scary. Business has never been more unpredictable, and that is very worrying because your whole livelihood depends on your success if you're running a business. I experienced having no money for seven years, and I can tell you, there was nothing more terrifying. Okay, nobody had died, but for me, being absolutely skint was the next worst thing.

Imagine it for a minute: you've got kids and you struggle to pay for their food, let alone their school uniforms, you lose your house, you have to watch all your friends and acquaintances on social media flaunting their tropical holidays and shiny new cars while you wonder if you'll survive the next month.

This might make the low bar bandwagon jumping very appealing. But it's a bad idea. As well as pointing you in the direction of what might end up being a very costly failure, it can also blind you to real opportunities.

You can go your own way – here's how

One rule that's always served me is don't follow the crowd. I listen carefully for people telling me I'm mad, because the thing they're advising against is usually the right way to go.

I'm not saying go out there and do something crazy that's a huge risk and guaranteed to fail. What I am saying is pause, engage brain and look at things differently to everyone else.

I wouldn't rule out something that's not sexy. Let's take retail as an example. Everyone is going online, jumping on the e-commerce bandwagon, joining the gold rush and looking for a piece of the action. I would take a step back and think about that. Where is retail unpopular and not in direct competition with the giants like Amazon? On the high street.

That was an unpopular idea, even before the COVID-19 pandemic. Now it's verging on mad. But look at companies that made a fortune during recessions: they went where they could pick up the bargains (take a look back at the examples in the chapter on companies launched in recessions). With the apparent collapse of the high street, properties are in low demand, which means rental costs are being driven down.

Almost everything can be done online today, without ever talking to another human face-to-face. But the more isolated people become because of the internet, the more valuable that real-life exchange is going to become. All you'd need is to identify something people need – a problem you can help them solve.

There are plenty of successful retailers not in direct competition with Amazon. Timpson is a great example, you can read all about that in the next chapter. And at the very top, you have prestigious companies like Selfridges, which appeal to a different demographic.

It's worth noting here that whatever the situation is today, it could be different tomorrow. Even the most successful companies have to change. Take the two examples I just used – Timpsons and Selfridges. Like all of us, both these companies had to adjust to survive the pandemic.

As bricks-and-mortar retail companies, they both had to close their doors and furlough staff. Timpsons got smart with finances and arranged an overdraft of £50 million as security. They stuck to their values – which include kindness – and topped up the government furlough pay-outs to staff so they all retained their full salaries while the doors were closed.

Selfridges, meanwhile, turned its attention to sustainability and focused on finding opportunities to try out new business models. One example is a 'clothing-as-a-service' offer, which lets customers rent the clothes rather than buying them.

This is what this book is all about. Sometimes you have to reinvent yourself, and you're not going to do it by taking the obvious, easy route. I won't try and sell you some magic formula to this, but there are a few clear steps I take that might help you.

1. **Look in the opposite direction.** In the late 1950s, my father passed a book down to me called *Strategy: The Indirect Approach*, by B. H. Liddell Hart. A short 1955 review on the Foreign Affairs website describes Liddell Hart's approach to strategy: 'frontal assaults and massive showdowns are to be avoided; rather one should aim at the enemy's line of least expectation.' I've always taken the indirect approach by looking at what everyone else is doing and going in the opposite direction. I think that's the first step: notice where everyone else is going and explore what the opposite of that is.

2. **Think.** This might seem obvious, but one of the reasons businesses often fail fast is that people don't think. I mean really think. It's something we rarely make time for because we're constantly multitasking, with one eye on the Facebook feed and another on incoming emails. Thinking means concentrating on something for long enough to come up with your own ideas about it, like solving a problem, for example. Thinking is a hugely underused skill, and it's something everyone can get better at. All you need to do is practice. My suggestion is to purposefully spend 15 minutes a day (at least) really thinking about an aspect of your reinvention, with no distractions. Take notes and you'll see where this takes you.

3. **Be sceptical.** If you walk into a car showroom and the salesperson tells you that the car will make you irresistible, it will drive at 200 miles an hour and it will go up in value, do you believe them? Of course not. Yet so many people believe what they read, fall for ads and throw their money after things they don't need and that don't work. This is often because the thing we're being sold – the product or service or idea – is something we want, that's convenient, easy, that makes us feel good about ourselves. Stop trying to feel better by believing everything and instead, question everything. You'll soon start to see a more realistic picture of the world, and that will open up opportunities for you.

It's always better to sidestep conventional wisdom, ignore advisors and do things your own way. Question everything. Explore everything. Talk to everyone. And when you're confident you know what's happening, make your move.

Fitting it all in

Feeling impatient? This isn't exactly a quick fix. If you want to do it right and succeed, reinvention takes time. But that doesn't mean you can't make a start right now, even if you're busy.

In chapter 6, we looked at why you need to just get started. Looking at what might be involved, the time investment could seem overwhelming. I think the key is to set up your life to make room for the reinvention, so it doesn't get pushed to one side or take over completely.

I tend to be somebody who does everything in a routine. Every morning I get up and cycle 25 miles, I come home, I have a shower. I drink my lovely espresso, which gives me a high, get in my car and go to my office. I work. I come home. I've been going on holiday to Portugal for the last 23 years – we stay at exactly the same place, we eat at the same restaurant, we do the same things. I've designed my life to include all the things that are most important to me. If there's a problem that needs solving, I schedule time for it. If there's a business opportunity to think about, I schedule time for it.

There's another reason for my almost obsessive scheduling: I don't like to be doing nothing. If I have a slot available, I like to fill it; I find the day goes much better if every timeslot is planned in advance. The worst thing to me is just sitting around doing nothing. That doesn't mean I'm always working – I might fill a gap with a game of Scrabble with a friend. What I don't want to end up doing is sitting in front of Netflix with a glass of wine. All that does is clouds my brain. I find that by scheduling everything carefully, I can better deal with stress and anxiety.

There's an old saying: Satan makes work for idle hands. I think anxiety will proliferate if you give it the breathing space. I've figured out that keeping my brain busy all the time works best for me. But I'm not an expert, so now I'm going to hand over to the king of compartmentalisation.

Rob: Routine = Results

Ha-ha, well, some have called me the king of compartmentalisation. I literally wrote the book on it!

I wrote *Routine = Results* because I know how powerful a solid routine can be for getting things done in your life. You need time and space to think and plan to reinvent yourself. Whatever sort of reinvention it is, you'll be investing some of your life into making it happen. And scheduling is your messy, unsexy path to success.

Everyone talks about the hustle and grind, the 5 am club, the push-yourself-to-breaking-point approach. None of that is necessary, and I happen to think it's straight up stupid to put yourself through all that unnecessarily. What's the point in burning out halfway through the journey? What's the point in humping the wrong tree, harder, harder, faster, faster?

Time management is a myth too – time isn't something you can change, you can't manage it, you can't bend it to fit your plans better. If that were possible, we'd all be slowing things down so we'd have a few seconds longer to smell the roses. We'd have 25 hours in a day (which most people would also waste). What you *can* manage is yourself, your activities and your diary. You can't manage time, but you can manage your life.

You might know this analogy already, but I'll go over it briefly because it's a really visual, understandable way of thinking about routine management.

On a table in front of you, there's a big empty glass jar. Next to the jar, there are a mound of rocks, a mound of pebbles and a mound of sand. You need to put the three mounds into the jar. How do you do it?

If you put the sand in first, the pebbles will sit on top, leaving you just enough room to squash in a single rock. But if you put the rocks in first, then the pebbles and then the sand, pebbles and sand will fall between the rocks and fill up the gaps, and lo and behold, it all fits in.

Now let's make these items represent things. The jar is your life. The rocks are the big non-negotiable things in your life – your family, your health: your KLAs (Key Life Areas). The pebbles are important things like IGTs (Income Generating Tasks), and other important areas to you that you could live without, but which are more important than admin and nice to be done when you have time – your career, your hobbies. The sand is the minutiae you could easily leave – watching TV and doing admin, reacting to other people's problems and emergencies, scrolling through social media.

Just like you put the rocks, pebbles and sand into the jar in a certain order to make them fit, you need to put your metaphorical rocks, pebbles and sand – your non-negotiable, important and optional tasks – into your life in the right order.

I bet you don't do it, though. It's simple, but not easy. To know and not to do, is not to know. The lure of the satisfaction of ticking something off the list all too often means pebbles and sand get addressed first, and rocks end up not fitting in at the end of it all. That does not create a happy, fulfilling life. You can't fill your jar with meaningful things if menial things are always filling it first.

Here's how to create a routine that gets you results – and a reinvention.

Compartmentalising your time

This is a really simple process. First, I'll talk through how to compartmentalise your time, then how to tweak your schedule to make it really work for you.

1. Name your rocks. You can imagine them like big smooth rocks with colourful pictures painted on them, if that helps. You don't need many, but you want to make sure you've identified all the rocks in your life. What is most important to you? What could you absolutely not live without? Think about family, health, maybe a hobby that makes your heart sing, walks with your dog, your vision, mission and passion, your reinvention. Literally name the rocks – if you can see them in your mind, you'll take them seriously.

2. Identify your pebbles. Your pebbles are important too, and they could be income generating, but they're not as vital as your rocks. You might find things like your career, friends, business and house here. Write a list of pebbles.

3. Identify your sand. What are the other things in your life, the little things you could do without but always seem to end up getting ticked off first? Write them down. This almost becomes a 'not to do' list, which, believe me, is just as important as a 'to do' list.

4. Get a year's worth of clear weekly calendar pages – you're going to start from scratch. Choose whatever format works best for you, whether that's a Google, Microsoft or iCal calendar or a hand-drawn masterpiece you'll put on the wall.

5. Add things in this order: rocks, pebbles, sand. Make sure you're realistic with the time each thing will take. At this stage, you're not looking at individual tasks, but projects and activities. So you might have a three-hour block on a Tuesday morning to work on your reinvention. Within that block, you can then set out the tasks you're going to complete, like developing your vision, planning, strategy, batching sales calls and so on. Set this calendar entry to recur each day, week, month – whatever works for you, as long as it's regular, it stays evergreen, and you DO NOT REMOVE IT.

I sometimes hear that people feel awkward about scheduling time they feel should be spontaneous. I mean, it is a bit awkward to schedule sexy time with your significant other (I totally recommend this though, it gives me something to look forward to all day, and it gives my wife enough time to… er… get ready… no comment, LOL).

The reality is that if you're disorganised and really busy, you won't make the time for those moments at all. I mentor many entrepreneurs who get so busy that all the things they love to do initially get put on the back burner temporarily, and in the end, they get dropped forever. I made this mistake, and I don't want you to make it too. If being spontaneous is important to you, block time and do something spontaneous within that time.

Start using the schedule, but realise it's not set in stone. The lid hasn't been glued onto your metaphorical glass jar. By monitoring how it's going and making changes, you can refine it over time and make it really work for you. I usually refine or tweak mine every three months. I also have a different version for the school holidays, so I can spend a lot more time with my kids.

There's so much more to routine, and so many ways you can use it to get results. It's about being clear on your KLAs, KRAs and IGTs, compartmentalising your diary, then being focused, disciplined and in flow to get each important job done, one by one, step by step. I also really value my variation on 80-20, which is the 70-20-10 method.

Using 70-20-10 to prioritise your reinvention

Whether you've made your reinvention a rock or a pebble (if it lands anywhere further down the pecking order, you might want to re-evaluate whether you really want to do it), you might want to incorporate it into your broader life strategy in the form of a 70-20-10 plan.

To illustrate this, let's take a business reinvention as an example. You're looking to branch out into a new area or start a new business. When you're busy working, it's very easy to get swept up in what needs to be done, and to prioritise what I call your income generating tasks (IGTs) so highly that your new ideas don't get a look in. Making a 70-20-10 plan overcomes this.

70-20-10 is a time division model, where you focus 70 percent of your time on your main strategy, 20 percent of your time on your secondary strategy, and 10 percent of your time on a third strategy, future project or research for something you want to try. This achieves several things, including two important ones: first, you give yourself the opportunity to work on the new stuff, and second, you spread your risk.

Let's imagine you're running a bakery (your main strategy). It's buzzing, you're the talk of the town, but you started to get bored – you had enough of fattening up the punters, you wanted to diversify. You set up a cake school (your secondary strategy). Your bakery needs most of your attention to keep running, but you can give 20 percent of your time and attention to the cake school.

There's this other thing too... calligraphy (your third strategy). You think it could fit – people who buy or make posh cakes might also need invitations or place names for tables at parties. If you give it 10 percent, you can test out your idea without losing much if it doesn't work out.

70 percent – bakery

20 percent – cake school

10 percent – calligraphy

In that simple plan, you've given your reinvention (branching out into calligraphy) the space, time and attention it needs. You can now paint cake school and calligraphy on a couple of rocks and take it all to the next level.

Timpson

In UK retail, one of the big success stories is Timpson – a very boring business in a niche that's – so far – untouched by the internet giants.

Timpson is where you go to have your shoes re-heeled, keys cut, pen engraved, sign made, padlock picked, watch battery changed... all the odds and ends that don't quite fit anywhere else. Success on the high street today happens when you can offer something customers can't get easily online, and all these services tick that box. This means Timpson is not (yet) in direct competition with Amazon.

Timpson is a family business that was founded more than 150 years ago. It is now being run by a fourth generation Timpson – James – in the CEO position, leading 2,000 stores in the UK. But it's James's father John, currently owner and chairman, who really made his mark on the retail market. Or, rather, Sir William John Anthony Timpson CBE.

Like me, Sir John Timpson didn't jump straight into top position at the company. He was put in charge of procurement when he joined in 1970. When the company was acquired by UDS Group three years later, he moved around in the subsidiary companies, leading different areas, such as leather and fur.

A decade later, he negotiated a £42 million management buyout that brought the company back to the family. He sold the shoe shops the company had acquired over the years and refocused on shoe repair and key cutting, broadening the services to include engraving and a few other things. But the real shake-up came when he turned the management model upside-down, putting customers at the top and managers at the bottom.

Timpson has said giving employees autonomy was the core of their success, but I think there's a lot more to it. For a start, Timpsons is the most unglamorous business you can imagine. But the central mission remains what it was more than a century ago, and fundamentally, that aspect of society hasn't changed: we still wear shoes, and we have no idea how to fix them. Sure, they've added other things to the portfolio and acquired different businesses along the way – including buying a chain of digital photo shops from Tesco in 2014 – but it's remained pretty reliable over the years.

What's notable is how this constant reinvention, done by incorporating new companies and services, has been so fluid, with such little fanfare. It's a plain company offering products and services we need, and by putting us – the customers – first, it has done remarkably well.

Even when other companies were panicking about shutting up shop during the pandemic lockdown, Timpson remained stoic in its approach. The company put a freeze on HR, which meant nobody was losing a job during the pandemic – not even those whose contracts were up for review. Many staff were furloughed, and Timpson topped up their pay to 100 percent. Instead of letting employees take the hit, the company itself has gone into a sizeable overdraft to protect its interests. So far, the tactic is working, and when shops reopened, staff morale was high.

To me, this is a great example of a company that goes its own way and doesn't jump on the bandwagon. First and foremost Timpson listens to customers, which I find critically important, and responds with changes to its offering. There's a website now, but there wasn't for a long time – nothing is done in order to run with the crowd.

This is a testament to Sir John Timpson's impressive strategic instinct. He's a figure I have looked up to for many years, so you can imagine how honoured I was when he included me in his book *High Street Heroes: The Story of British Retail in 50 People*. He described me as 'bold, ambitious, innovative, using aggressive marketing to put jewellery shopping within everyone's budget. Few people have had as much influence on the shape of our high street.'

Back in 2015, he told the *Independent* that 'Bricks and mortar is still the future... I'm not convinced yet that online retailers will ever make money; the supermarkets are losing about £100 million on their internet services. Just wait and see – there will soon be new retailers we don't know about yet who will lead the next generation. Bring them on.'

I wonder what his post-COVID-19 thoughts on this would be. In early 2020, he said he expected the high street to look 'somewhat different' post-lockdown, but I bet whatever happens, he won't be going with the crowd.

Timeline: Sir William John Anthony Timpson CBE

1943: born

1950s-60s: Oundle School, Nottingham University

1960s: Career Graduate Trainee with Clarks in Street, Somerset

1970: Director of Buying at Timpson

1975: Managing Director of William Timpson

1983: Led company buyout from UDS Group (£42 million)

1987: Sold shoe shops, expanded to shoe repair and key cutting

1995: Acquired Automagic (120-shop chain)

2004: CBE for services to the retail sector

2014: Acquired 139 digital photo shops from Tesco

2017: Knighted for services to business and fostering

2019: Estimated net worth – £210 million

CHAPTER 9
Build a Support System

I was lying on a sun lounger by the pool with a cocktail in my hand when my phone rang. I looked at the number – London. I let it ring a few times, then answered. It was a city journalist at *The Telegraph* asking about my plans to get back into jewellery.

'No comment,' I said, and took a sip of my drink.

Every year, 1.8 million Brits travel to Portugal on holiday, and every year, I'm one of them. But it wasn't always that way. After The Speech, in my seven years of being jobless, depressed and skint, there was no way to go on holiday. That's a situation a lot of people are familiar with – maybe you're one of them.

It's a first world problem, of course, but it had a significant impact on me. Holidays were always my way to decompress, to relax. Running a business is stressful, and everyone needs to find a way to cope with that stress. Holidays were always one of my coping mechanisms.

When I was rebuilding my life and working on the health club, I was fully focused on making it a success. I wasn't going to take my foot off the accelerator until I knew it would end well. I knew it was the right thing to do when I sold the club, and the relief was huge. Part of that relief was financial – I could offset the £1 million tax I'd paid against the £3.9 million I was making by selling the business. So not only did I get the money from the sale, but also the tax money. It was an incredible feeling.

And it was the first time I went on holiday in seven years.

I could finally let go and relax. I had enough money to make us comfortable again, and I had proven to myself that I could be successful in business.

I was already making plans to start Gerald Online, but I needed a break before pushing on with it.

Plus, selling a business you've personally built from nothing (literally) is a big career move – one that warrants celebration. I think this is an important part of the reinvention process – you mark the moment you shifted something, you reflect, look back at what has happened and look forward to what comes next.

That holiday was fabulous. I felt like me again. We were finally back on track; Moira was happy, and we were enjoying some stress-free time together.

There's a restaurant in the Algarve with panoramic views of the shimmering blue Atlantic Ocean. The coast-facing side of the restaurant is glass from floor to ceiling, framing the view like a painting. The sea reflects the clear blue of the cloudless sky, and tufts of green jut out of the sandy terrain. Together, those few colours and textures are breath-taking. They've kept us coming back for more than two decades.

The food is great at that restaurant, but what makes it really special is the carefree breeze that wisps among the sun kissed holidaymakers. Everyone is chatting and clinking glasses and taking a breather from the stress in their lives. And they're all snapping every moment on their phones, keen to share (or show off) their little bit of paradise.

One of the things that contributed to my depression after my downfall was watching everyone around me flaunting their success. At least it felt that way. All I saw was their flashy cars, glitzy nights out, sunny holidays, second homes. Of course that's all I saw – it was all they were showing me.

In reality, I was only seeing the cherries on top – the good bits of their lives. I was comparing the depths of my despair to the peaks of their happiness. With the advantage of hindsight, I can now see that it wasn't a fair comparison, but at the time I didn't see the difference. All the lights of everyone's success only cast a darker shadow over my own failure.

This comparison is something we're wired to do as humans, and it can be helpful. If we're looking up to people who inspire us, it can help us close the gap – to develop in a positive direction. But more often it ends up being destructive.

There came a moment when I realised if I carried on the way I was going – in bed, in front of Countdown, tea in one hand, biscuit in the other – I would never feel the sparkle all these people were enjoying. When Moira gave me that kick, what kept me moving forward was the idea that if I didn't change, I'd never get back what they had, and what I once had.

I'm grateful for one thing in particular: this was years before Facebook and Instagram came along. Back then, people used to be relatively discreet about their success. Now, they're being flaunted, they're right in your face. The false comparison effect is far worse today – social media has given us the opportunity to compare ourselves with everyone, usually with no context and little reality.

Something else I can now see clearly in hindsight is that the people I was comparing myself to so painfully weren't my real friends at all. It's incredible how fast I lost most of my 'friends' when I lost my job at Ratners. People say you know who your friends are when you hit rock bottom. Well I certainly didn't get invited to Buckingham Palace or 10 Downing Street anymore after I lost all my money.

As I slowly rebuilt my life, I also rebuilt my network. There were a lot of people in and around my life at the time that were influencing me in various ways. I knew that if I was going to be successful again, I would need to whittle that group down to people I could trust, people I could look up to and people who believed in me.

You become those you spend the most time with

It's been written and said a hundred different ways, but I think there's a lot of wisdom in this idea: if you look at the handful of people you spend the most time with, you'll see their behaviour and attitudes reflected in your own. When you're reinventing yourself, it's vital that you construct a strong support network around you.

Two of the people who have had the biggest influence on my career are Charles Saatchi and Michael Green. They were always looking at business in international terms – they had success in America, where the market for jewellery is 50 times bigger than it is in the UK. In the 1980s, Charles and Michael didn't do me any favours business-wise – I was ultimately in danger of overexpanding and doing too much.

But the real influence they had on me, the biggest positive effect they had on my life, was more to do with mindset. Hearing about everything they were achieving in America, about how fast their businesses were growing, and seeing their drive and conviction that they would be successful made me believe I could achieve anything.

I was in my 30s – young and ambitious. I spent more and more time with Charles and Michael, most often playing snooker. I started thinking beyond running a chain of jewellers; I wanted to have an international business and have thousands of stores. Spending time with them made me realise you don't just sit around and accept what you've got. There are opportunities, and those opportunities are there for everybody.

Charles Saatchi had no fear whatsoever about anything; he had balls of steel. He put an art gallery in a 50,000-square-foot building on Abbey Road in London. Who would start a private art gallery like that? There was already the Tate and the National Gallery, who's got the guts to suddenly take a massive great big warehouse and build a gallery? He had the sort of outlook on life that made him positive that he could open up an art gallery of that size. Nobody does that, but he did it.

That's what influenced me – the idea that you can do anything you want and go your own way. They also showed me that it's not as difficult as people think it is. The main thing is taking the first step; the biggest mistake is to sit back and say it's too risky.

Know when to ignore advice

In the last chapter, I wrote about why I go against the grain and do the opposite of what everyone else is doing. I mentioned that part of that means going ahead with things when people tell me I'm crazy.

I make light of it a bit, but this isn't an easy thing to do. One of the benefits of having a strong support system is that we can lean on them for their perspectives, expertise and experience. The result of that is we are all flooded with advice from everyone around us. This changes throughout our lives – as children, we're guided closely, and that guidance becomes more hands-off and more specific as we grow up.

You can see the same pattern throughout your career. At the beginning, everyone has advice, and you can often make progress by following it. But the further you get, the higher up the ladder, the more you rely on your own growing expertise.

In terms of knowledge, it's a good idea to look to others for advice – they can fill the gaps you have. But it's important to recognise when you need to lean on knowledge and when you need to trust your own intuition.

Some of the worst decisions I made in business have happened when I've taken too much advice. My own stockbroker once talked me out of a deal where I could buy 600 stores in America called Gordon's. He warned me that the Ratners share price would fall after the deal, and I accepted it as a reason not to go ahead.

But if I'd thought about it more from my perspective, I would have seen that while the shares would drop in value in the short term, the deal would have grown the company – and its value – significantly in the long term.

In that situation, my stockbroker was giving me advice he really believed was good; from his perspective, the short-term value for shareholders was the most important thing. But he was giving me advice based on what suited him. He even put pressure on the company's shareholders to agree.

This is an important consideration in business: public companies are all about short-term quarterly profits and fast growth. Of course, this can lead to collapse, and we see that all too often, but the cycle continues – the aim is to make the biggest return for shareholders.

The advice to stop the 600-store deal wasn't the only time a stockbroker advised me to do something in the short-term interests of shareholders. Being young and naive, I was easily egged on to push for fast growth rather than think strategically for the long term.

I've since learned to be wary of people's motives when they give advice – that's the first thing to consider. The fact that it's advice based on conventional wisdom also raises a red flag for me: I tend to go against that now. Does it annoy people? Yes. Do I care? No.

Get brilliant at hiring people

One area I've always been good at and tended to go my own way regardless of advice is hiring staff. At the health club, we wanted to start a spa area where you could have beauty treatments. I needed to find good staff to run that new area. Everyone was saying 'you must go and visit the famous Clifton hotel'; they were charging a fortune for their spa treatments.

So I went over there, and they had very, very good staff. But they were all unhappy in their jobs – and that gave me an advantage. I invited five of them to come and work for me for more money, because I knew they'd be better looked after, and get more job satisfaction with us. That's exactly what happened: they all accepted my offer and soon we had a fantastic spa area with the five best therapists around working in it.

I might be good at motivating people, or looking ahead to predict how business will go and what direction to take it in, but I'm not an expert in every particular area of the business. That means I have to get very good at one thing: hiring the right people.

The bigger the business gets, the truer this becomes. If you're reinventing yourself by starting a new business, you might be in a position where you're starting on your own. You have to be the CEO, CFO, marketing manager, business development VP, salesperson and tech support. If you're great at one thing you're probably not very good at another thing; I don't believe that anybody is an all-rounder who is brilliant at everything.

You've got to know what you're good at, and when the time is right, start handing out the tasks that don't land in your area of expertise to other people. In my case, it was marketing, morale boosting and strategy: I have always been good at looking ahead at where the company is going. But choosing the right products to sell? Forget it. Since that was the most important thing at Ratners, I had to be sure to hire the best buyers.

We had a buyer called Henry. He had the most terrible way about him, he wasn't at all personable, he was extremely scruffy, and he smoked like a chimney. He always had a cigarette in his mouth and the ash would drop into his cup of tea, it was really quite revolting. But he was an outstanding buyer, much better than the smooth operators in the double-breasted suits. He could pick out the exact products we needed, that would suit our customers and fly off the shelves. To use my racing analogy, he was a good horse, over the right distance.

I want to mention Timpson again here. Speaking at an entrepreneurs' conference in May 2018, Sir John Timpson said that after 20 years of running high street giant Timpson, he discovered the secret to great customer service: you have to trust your employees who serve them. It's not about training or processes or management, it's about empowering people to act autonomously. He even gives staff the freedom to hand out discounts.

The key, he says, is to hire for personality. Because you can teach someone to cut keys and repair shoes, but you can't change their personality.

'It's very simple. I'm not interested in what qualifications they've got, I don't care whether they've got letters after their name, I don't care what they put on their application form. I just want the right personality.'

I love their approach to recruitment. The interviewer has a sheet to fill in that features all the Mr. Men characters – Happy, Nosey, Lazy, Funny and so on – and tick the personality traits that most closely match the candidate. Then the candidate goes to work in a shop for half a day to see how they fit in the working environment.

This approach relies on the quality of the company's training, and by bringing in people who fit the culture, it supports their aim to give employees autonomy. The result is that if someone stays for two years, they're pretty likely to stay for two decades.

I pride myself on providing a positive working environment too. The morale, which is very important to business, has always been sky high at my companies, and people always love working for me. Still today I get loads of messages from people who used to work for me, sharing the success they've had in their careers.

'Doing a Ratner' on social media

I know how it is to work at my companies, so I get very upset when I'm criticised for being a bad boss. Because it simply isn't true. For some reason, this is one of the false criticisms I face regularly on Twitter (as if there isn't anything true, they can criticise me for).

In hindsight, having an attitude boost from Charles and Michael in particular gave me some resilience against the backlash that was headed my way on social media in the early days.

The fact that I built the world's largest jewellery business, made millions of pounds with the health club business and started one of the first successful online jewellery companies seems to fade into insignificance on Twitter.

Instead, since The Speech, I've been a target for criticism and downright nastiness.

There are so many things that people could say about me. For one thing, few people make a fortune once, and even fewer do it twice. Instead, I'm the poster boy for failure on Twitter.

Whenever someone screws up in a big way, people start talking about the Gerald Ratner School of this and that, or they say that the person 'did a Ratner'. These are not once-in-a-blue-moon occurrences; somebody does a Ratner, according to Twitter, twice a week. This is not a legacy that I wanted. But I live with it and I've had to learn to accept it.

I'll be honest, though, I haven't always been accepting about it. I tend to shoot my mouth off before engaging my brain. I really lose my temper sometimes and react to things. It's almost always a bad idea, but it does entertain people. I'm the first to admit I've made some terrible mistakes in dealing with critics online. When you think about it, this is still a relatively new world – like many people, I'm still working out the best way to deal with the constant judgement. (Rob's got a lot of good stuff to say on this.)

The people who are really nasty on Twitter are that way because their lives are miserable, and they want everybody else to be miserable. Once upon a time, you'd only really see this at the pub, where they'd have to square up to you and say things to your face. On social media, particularly Twitter, people have free reign to vent their anger, and there's some real nastiness out there.

One of the causes of so-called trolling online is a kneejerk reaction to comparison. There's a misguided mentality that if you are completely skint, for example, it's going to be better for you if somebody else is skint too. This is complete and utter rubbish, of course, because it makes no difference whatsoever. But unfortunately, that's an attitude you encounter frequently online: if I can't be successful, nobody else can. This is reflected in people's behaviour – it comes out as abuse.

The thing that bothers me most about the abuse I get on Twitter is what people choose to attack me for. If they were gunning for my diplomacy or ability to always say the right thing, I'd hold my hands up – I'm the first to admit I tend to not know when to keep my mouth shut. But it's almost always my management skills that come into question. My ability to run a successful business. My approach to marketing. The very things that I'm good at. If they're going to criticise me, they really should try to get it right.

This isn't just irritating; it's also potentially damaging to my business. When people falsely claim that I've gone bust again, it can start a rumour that puts me in a difficult position with suppliers; with a damaged reputation, you can't buy diamonds.

Although I'm unpopular with people who don't know me on Twitter, I'm very popular on social media among people who have worked for me and people who have heard my speeches, especially on LinkedIn and Facebook. It's exactly the opposite situation – night and day. Knowing I've made a positive impact on people's lives as their employer, or inspired them with a speech I've given, is enough to lift my spirits regardless of the critics.

It's a sad reality, but this is something you'll need to consider when you're reinventing yourself. If you're fortunate, your reinvention will go down brilliantly with everyone and you'll be showered with positive messages. Or maybe you'll choose to do it quietly rather than publicly. But if you are planning to be online, to be exposed to people on social media, it's a good idea to steel yourself against critics, haters and trolls. Rob will have some practical advice on this at the end of the chapter.

If your reinvention is really going to be in the public eye, you might have to prepare for the next-level critics: the press.

Staying on the right side of the press

Thirty years ago, if you made a big mistake in business, you wouldn't get roasted on social media, but it would be plastered across the headlines.

That's a humiliation I hope you're spared. One move I've managed to get wrong a few times is to react badly to criticism doled out by journalists. That isn't good business, because journalists are very important.

Looking back to 1991, one of my big mistakes was fighting against the press when the story about The Speech came out. I'd always had a good relationship with journalists, and this took me down a path that wasn't sensible to follow. I now realise that it's much better to own up to your mistakes, don't argue with the judgement. People will be much more sympathetic.

The reasons I've always got along well with journalists are that I'm honest and I'm not political. We've had a good rapport in the past. Even in the midst of the furore in 1991, the city journalists I knew well were apologetic about everything that was happening. The coverage had nothing to do with them – it had crept out of the city section and onto the news pages, where the hacks were less than forthcoming with empathy and kindness.

I had been warned about journalists early on in my career. People told me to be careful about how closely I worked with them and how much I trusted them; I was told they were only building me up to knock me down. I poo-pooed that – it's an overused expression, for one thing – and in many ways, I was right.

When I tried to buy H. Samuel, the press was positive about the move. I used that to my advantage – I orchestrated some press coverage in the *Telegraph* about my intention to buy the company before it was even a possibility. In the end, it resulted in support from the chairman of H. Samuel, and a successful sale.

The story behind the sale is that I had bought 27 percent of the company from – you'll never guess – the chairman's mother. She had seen the article and it had convinced her it was a good idea. The rest just followed from there; three months later I'd sacked the chairman and was in charge of a significantly more powerful company.

Being accessible worked to my advantage with the press. I'm not the kind of person who sits in their ivory tower, and that got them some very useful and direct stories form me over the years. Yet when the tide turned, that's where they all painted me – in my ivory tower, far away from the customers I cared so much about.

I was disappointed, humiliated and angry when the stories hit after The Speech. It felt like a betrayal, and it was such a non-story – I'd made those jokes before, all they did was grab them from the wrong angle.

The day after I lost my job, one journalist called me, nice as pie (they always are after they've roasted you in black and white). I remember him telling me that cream in a coffee always rises to the top. I was confused at first, but what he meant was that I had success within me, I had done it before, and he believed I would make a comeback. I might have lost my job, and everything else, but it wasn't because I was bad at my job, it was because I was bad at making jokes.

That was comforting at times, and occasionally I still think back to that call. When you're in the public eye, a lot of the people around you will be gunning for you – they'll be looking for ways to beat you down, pick you apart, chew you up and spit you out, all in the name of entertainment. Like it or not, they're part of your life. What strengthens your support system is finding the good among the bad and holding on to the positivity that emerges. Because it always does.

Incidentally, I recently found out that the journalist who broke the story that led to my downfall had been telling colleagues for months that he was going to get revenge. Why? Apparently, his nephew had been sacked from one of my shops. The fact that I employed 25,000 people (more than the Royal Navy) and had never met or even heard of him, let alone had anything to do with his dismissal, didn't seem to matter. According to my source, the proprietor of *The Daily Mirror* at the time, Robert Maxwell, spurred him on. After seeing the story in the *Mirror,* *The Sun* changed their headline. The rest, as they say, is history.

Rob: build a strong support scaffold

I don't envy Gerald. I get my fair share of hate online, but he makes me look like the Dalai Lama. Gerald was really dragged through the mud – and some. The fact that he continues to talk to the people who criticised him shows his ability to reinvent himself and move on from his past, how much belief he has in himself, and how much forgiveness he has in other people.

Whatever happens, you can't give up on humanity. If Gerald had done that, he'd still be in bed – probably alone, and in a much smaller house. I think Countdown is still on too, so he'd still be watching that. Like it or not, your reinvention depends on other people. If you're going to make it through this process, you need human scaffolding, built up in layers: family and friends, peers, heroes, coaches and mentors. And in the basement: your critics, haters and trolls. These are people you should choose very carefully.

Family and friends

If you're scheduling your life rocks-first, you're already on your way to strengthening this layer of your support scaffold. These are the people who are closest to you in your life, they are the ones who will love you no matter what happens. They're your cheerleaders, your unconditional supporters. Give them a rock. Some people have conflict within their family, others have family they don't like. You can't choose your family, but in instances where you don't have support, you need to be mindful of how much time you spend with people who haven't got your back, even if you're related.

Peers

These are people who are on your level in some way or area of life – most likely in work or business. They might be colleagues, friends in business or entrepreneurs, or they could be working for or running other companies (maybe your competition). These are people you can talk to about your daily issues, who you can ask for advice and bounce ideas around with.

People you have a lot in common with. People you trust and respect. I especially like keeping competitors as friends; that gives you an advantage over most, as people tend to get defensive around competition.

Heroes

Who are your heroes? These are the people you aspire to be like. You might look up to certain character traits or physical abilities, to their business acumen or music skills. Usually your heroes will be out of arm's reach – they're real, but they act more like guiding stars in the distance. You might connect with them through books (I read a lot of autobiographies), social media, podcasts or YouTube. As you grow, you will catch up with your heroes. I've been lucky enough to meet most of mine. Just be careful not to over pedestalise them: they are human and flawed just like you and I, too.

Coaches

These are people who hold your hand and ask you questions to help you make good decisions. They're great motivators, but they're not necessarily experts in what you're doing, or the direction you're heading in. We all need a shot in the arm, pat on the back or kick up the arse from time to time, and coaches are the best for that.

Mentors

When you get a mentor, you're investing in someone who has been in your position in years gone by, who's one or more steps ahead of you and who can help guide you in the right direction. They come in different shapes and sizes: they could be the biggest in your industry, at the top of their game, a retired expert or a successful business owner or entrepreneur. I think you get what you pay for when it comes to mentors.

The basement

I'm including this in your scaffolding because I think there's almost always some value to criticism you get, even if it's utter bollocks and merely serves to thicken your skin. There's often truth in criticism, if you're balanced and wise to see it. If someone is criticising you, see if you can take something from it – something to help you improve. If they're hating you, kill them with kindness. Have fun and banter with them. Or ignore them if that's too hard. And trolls? Block or report them. You can always leave your fans to stick up for you with the basement brigade.

Why mentors are so important

I'm a massive believer in standing on the shoulders of giants – not just learning from their mistakes, as we've already covered, but also spring-boarding from their wins. Look at any successful person and you'll find a mentor behind them. Oprah had Maya Angelou, Mark Zuckerberg had Steve Jobs, Bill Gates had Warren Buffet, I've had Mark Homer, Warren Borsje, Andreas Panayiotou, James Caan, John Demartini… (I'm the first to admit I'm a bit of a mentor whore.)

This is one really important element I think is too often missing. Everyone needs a mentor, especially if you're going through a reinvention. You need someone who has been there, who has gone through what you're facing and come out the other side.

I hear a lot of people moaning about mentors costing money, and to be honest, I think that's a bit ridiculous. Firstly, when you're thinking about mentorship, the cost shouldn't be the consideration, it's the return on investment you need to look at. If you're investing a couple of thousand a month in a mentor who will help you make ten grand a month, that to me is a no-brainer.

I have first-hand experience. When I was still working at the pub, directionless and penniless, I hadn't ever considered finding a mentor – I wouldn't have had a clue where to look. I didn't really understand the concept, and I guess I was too proud to ask. I felt I just had to get my head down and figure stuff out for myself. The problem is you don't know what you don't know.

When I met Mark Homer at a networking event and we started some property partnerships, we used to get lunches with millionaires, even the occasional billionaire. We were constantly on the lookout for people who had been where we wanted to go, and when we found them, we chewed their ears off with questions.

You get to live vicariously through your mentors and learn from their successes, experiences and failures. Sorry to say this Gerald, but I'd rather watch you make that bad joke a hundred times than make it myself. I've enjoyed getting to know you over the years and I've learned a lot from your misery (I mean experience). ;-)

Gerald and I both mentor people and we both have mentors, so we know the system from every direction. Gerald is a mentor in one of my mastermind programmes, 'Business Mastermind Academy', with Kiddicare founder Neville Wright. Something Gerald has said to me before is that when you have a mentoring session, you go back to how things used to be – you sit down together and have an in-depth conversation.

That's really refreshing today, when people can't even seem to sit across a pub table from each other without screens getting in the way. And it highlights one thing: business has always been about people. Having interesting and challenging conversations with smart and experienced people really is one of the greatest ways to transcend any problem, and one of my single favourite things to do in life.

Avoid echo chambers

I've focused on a few layers for your support system here, but you're also constantly surrounded by people – at the supermarket, in the pub, at work, on the bus, in the playground at your kid's school – so you have loads of opportunity to meet new people and learn from them (I'll come back to that in chapter 10).

The wider you make the outer circles of your life – the friends, friends of friends, acquaintances, and so on – the more you'll be exposed to new opinions, perspectives and ideas. It's far too easy to create an echo chamber for yourself, especially online. People like you will like you. You will like, and feel comfortable, around people like you. The algorithms on many social media platforms will show you the things and the people you already have a connection too or something in common with, who you agree with and whose values you align with. It will literally feed you exactly who and what you want to see, and your ego will be fed too.

That won't help you grow. You don't need to be told what you already know. You don't need mindless agreement or sycophants. You need to disrupt your circles.

If you're 40 years old, seek out people who are 20. I do this – it keeps me feeling young and fresh and energetic. And I love having mentors who are 60 and older, because they are way wiser and way more experienced in life than I am, and they've seen a lot more.

Do this with all sorts of characteristics – location, culture, religion, politics, education, language. The broader you make your horizons, the more interesting the people you meet will be.

Hanging out with different people keeps you challenging your own beliefs, fears, doubts and mindsets. And, of course, through osmosis, you can learn a lot from them. That's going to be really valuable for your reinvention.

Mae Jemison

We've seen how the internet makes it not only possible but fast, easy and free to reinvent yourself. But what if the reinvention you're considering is more traditional and requires you to take a formal educational route? This will most likely be the case for professions like law and medicine, for example.

It is possible. It might not be easy, but if you're up for some hard work, there's no reason you can't do it. According to the Association of American Medical Colleges (AAMC), between 2000 and 2020, 1,143 medical students aged 40 or over graduated. That's just 0.3 percent of the total number of graduates. Small percentage though it is, to me, this says it's very possible to retrain in a high-pressure environment like medicine.

Many doctors go on to retrain in other fields too – like 'super scientist' Dr. Mae Jemison.

Jemison was already showing signs of being a polymath as a child, with a keen interest in space exploration, biology and dance. She was busy with various extracurricular activities at school, including ballet and cheerleading. She went to Stanford University at the age of just 16 and left with degrees in African and African-American studies, and chemical engineering. She went on to complete a medical degree at Cornell University before joining the Peace Corps as a doctor.

With the Peace Corps, Dr. Jemison travelled to Liberia and Sierra Leone, where she treated patients from 1983 to 1985. During that time, she was in charge of the lab, the pharmacy and the medical staff, as well as health and safety. All the while she was working as a doctor, she continued to take dance classes.

On her return to the US, Dr. Jemison wanted to fulfil her childhood dream, so she applied to NASA. The Challenger tragedy that happened in 1986 paused the program, so she reapplied and was accepted in 1987. Dr.

Jemison was one of 15 people chosen out of 2,000 applicants, becoming the first black woman astronaut.

She spent the next two years working at NASA, supporting launches and verifying software. Then, in 1989, she joined the crew of the Space Shuttle Endeavour mission (STS-47) as Mission Specialist 4 and Science Mission Specialist – a new role in which she would run scientific experiments.

In 1992, Dr. Jemison fulfilled her childhood dream: she went to space, from 12 to 22 September, and orbited the Earth 127 times.

On her return to Earth, Dr. Jemison would go through yet another reinvention and become an entrepreneur. She left NASA in 1993 and set up consulting firm The Jemison Group Inc., which brings socio-cultural issues into the design of engineering and science projects. The following year, she established the Dorothy Jemison Foundation for Excellence, and launched The Earth We Share (TEWS) – a science camp for teenagers.

Dr. Jemison went on to become Bayer Corporation USA's national science literacy ambassador, a member of the US National Academy of Medicine, Founding Chair of the Texas State Product Development and Small Business Incubator Board, an inductee of the National Women's Hall of Fame, and the recipient of a huge number of awards and accolades across science, medicine and business. Oh, and she was the first real astronaut to appear on the Star Trek TV series, as if all that wasn't impressive enough.

If you're doubting whether you can switch careers, retrain or try something new, get some inspiration from Dr. Mae Jemison – doctor, Peace Corps officer, NASA astronaut and scientist, entrepreneur, board member and television star.

CHAPTER 10
Design Your Own Education

They say your life flashes before you when you die. Well, I can tell you something similar happens when you walk onto the stage at the Royal Albert Hall to relive the moment that caused your downfall. As I stepped up to the podium, to the sound of enthusiastic and expectant applause, I was nervous. And this time it felt very real; I had spent the previous 14 years going over and over the worst-case scenario.

I took a sip of water and composed myself. I knew my speech inside out – I was going to talk about what had gone wrong there on the stage more than a decade before. I was going to talk about my fall, my comeback with the health club, and now, my relaunch into the jewellery business.

I had written some jokes into the speech – I've always loved to make people laugh – but they were very (very) carefully composed. They were self-deprecating, and I tested them out on just about everyone I'd spoken to in the weeks leading up to the event, so I knew they couldn't be taken the wrong way. I could picture the city journalists lines up outside salivating, just waiting for me to make a wrong move.

Despite the nerves, I was excited. I remembered how much I enjoyed public speaking, how fulfilling it was to make people laugh. I quickly got into a flow and I was away, it was natural. My worst nightmare didn't happen again. I had faced my fear and not only survived, but in that moment figured out what I really wanted to do.

I love public speaking. I adore it. When I get an email or a call inviting me to give a speech, I really look forward to it. I love turning up in London or Sunderland or Birmingham or even jumping on a plane somewhere – the new places, the people, all wanting to learn something from me.

I've done about 5,000 speeches since my comeback at the Royal Albert Hall – I've been known to speak three times on a single day. It's ironic, really – it was doing a speech, making people laugh, that got me into trouble in the first place, and it turns out that's actually my calling in life. But when I think about it, it makes perfect sense.

When I give a speech, I talk about The Speech. I go back over the misplaced (and misunderstood) jokes. The backlash from the press. The downward spiral at Ratners. Being sacked, spending years in darkness, then finally rebounding. It's cathartic; talking, reliving and joking about it has helped me bury this traumatic event.

It also continually reminds me that people are far nicer face-to-face than they are online (especially on Twitter), that it's better to stay connected rather than hiding away when things get hard. When I speak, I get such a fabulous reception – people are enthusiastic, they want to hear what I have to say. They ask questions, take selfies, say nice things.

And the biggest benefit of all is the fact that I can use my downfall as a learning tool – for me, just as much as for other people.

For me, speaking has meant I've had 5,000 opportunities to go over what happened, to analyse the whole story. You might think I did that constantly for seven years after it all happened, but that wasn't me analysing and learning, it was me wallowing. I didn't learn a thing by sitting there feeling sorry for myself.

Instead, when I talk through it with people, I see the situation from a different angle. It helps to have decades of time in between – that reduces the sting of embarrassment – but the change comes more from having to convert my direct experience into a story to share. I've heard this from many people, that telling their personal story helped them work through it and learn from it. This isn't just the case for giving speeches either, it also helps to write it all down, which I'm doing in part again here.

The rehashing of the story takes me part of the way, and it's the interaction with the audience that pushes me further. When people ask questions, they often help me learn something new about my own experience. They see it from their perspective, with their unique experience and knowledge, and their insights can be just as fascinating to me as my story is to them.

And of course, the audience learns too: they get to live through my downfall vicariously and learn from my mistakes without having to make any themselves. As I mentioned in chapter 3, failure is a great learning tool, but if you get the chance to piggyback on someone else's, for goodness sake take it.

There is another, rather more personal angle to the speeches: I get to put people right about who I am. For years, people have been getting the wrong idea about me, from articles saying I don't care about customers to tweets calling out my bogus failings as a manager. I don't put them right by blowing my own trumpet, though, I put them right by talking about all my mistakes. And the best part is I make them laugh in the process.

People prefer to hear a speech about calamities and disasters, because that's life. Have you ever met somebody who seems to sail through life, without any setbacks? There's an instant lack of empathy there. To really identify with someone's experience, you both need to have suffered somehow. I have suffered, make no mistake, and I'm better for it. And I think the audience share that. To turn the biggest corporate gaffe of all time to my advantage shows everyone that it's possible to turn their problems around. That's what people really want: possibility and hope.

There's always a line of people waiting to speak to me after a speech. They thank me for inspiring them or simply cheering them up. One person might talk about being on the verge of making a big business decision, another about to lose their home. There are all sorts of people listening and getting something out of my talk.

Listening to what they say reinforces the fact that I can help so many more people by standing on stage in front of a crowd than I can in conversation with individuals. That means a lot to me. I feel it's my responsibility to repay the business world, which overall has been good to me, by sharing my experiences and knowledge.

The story continues to evolve as time passes. Eighteen months after my first return to the Royal Albert Hall, I was back there again, in front of much the same crowd. By then, I had almost gone full circle, having taken Gerald Online to more than £20 million in sales.

Listen and learn

The irony of me now being a professional speaker is that I never used to bother going to conferences. I thought they were a total waste of time. I'd always preferred to learn by doing, and in my mind, I could be out there making money rather than listening to what someone else had to say. I was traveling at 100 miles an hour, I didn't have time to slow down at the lights, let alone pull over in a layby.

These days if I'm speaking at a conference, I'll enjoy the other talks and I always learn at least one thing. It takes concentration; you don't learn anything just from mid-air, you have to really listen.

Back in chapter 5, I shared some of my tips for keeping your brain healthy; a lot of these involve listening as a way of learning. I regularly listen to audiobooks and podcasts, for example. That's a great thing to incorporate into your life to make sure you're continuously learning. But to really learn, you need to extend those listening skills. It's not enough to stick a podcast on while you're cleaning up after dinner, or to listen to an audiobook while you're working out. That quickly turns into passive listening; what really makes a difference is active listening.

When I give a speech, I can tell who's going to get the most out of it: it's the people who listen carefully, maybe even take notes, then ask questions they don't yet know the answer to and really pay attention to what I say.

On the other side of the fence are the people who want to be right there with me on the podium. Their hands fly up the second they get the opportunity, and the questions that come out of their mouths are more like mini speeches they'd prepared in advance. And if they do ask questions, they usually pre-empt the answer, answer for me or even tell me why I'm wrong. That's their prerogative, of course – it's a speech, not a university lecture. But I think they're missing a really good opportunity to learn.

I'm sure you've come across this kind of person, and if you're honest, you've probably been this person at least once. I know I have, especially in my younger days. What I've learned over the years is that there's a lot of wisdom in the old adage that listening and speaking should happen in a two-to-one ratio; we have two ears and one mouth for a reason.

Active listening doesn't always come naturally, but it's something you can learn. Since we're talking about learning, here are a few steps you can take.

1. **Pay attention to what people say.** Put your phone away, stop watching the television over their shoulder. When you're having a conversation with someone, or listening to them speak, try to block out all distractions. I find it helps to imagine the situation with tunnel vision – focus on the other person and think about what they're saying. Actively process their words as you hear them. If you do this, your body language will naturally show you're listening (so none of this tilt your head to the side nonsense).

2. **Make sure you understand them.** One of the big causes of miscommunication is people half listening to one another and letting their own experiences and assumptions fill in the gaps. That's not helpful if your aim is to learn from what you're hearing. There are some great ways to make sure you understand, and the added bonus is that they stop you from interjecting with your own stories. You can summarise what they've said or repeat words or phrases back to them. Even better: ask open ended questions if there are things you want to clarify or explore.

3. **Respond, but don't interrupt.** There's one really important thing here that will help you stick to the two-to-one ratio: if your brain starts trying to come up with a response before they've even finished speaking, shut it up. You're not volleying; you want their words to hit you straight on. Instead, listen, clarify, then pause before you speak. You'll find it makes for a much more interesting conversation for you both.

When you develop good listening skills, you'll find you can apply them anywhere, which means you can turn every encounter you have into a learning opportunity. And that's what really makes a difference when you're reinventing yourself.

Your reinvention curriculum

When I started the health club, I was already on the road to becoming an expert in the business: I was cycling every day and working out, I'd joined a gym myself and I was convinced of the benefits of being healthy. But I still had a lot to learn.

This is likely to be true for anyone about to change direction in life. A reinvention almost always requires some kind of new skill or knowledge. If you don't acquire it before you start (or, as we saw in chapter 6, get started and learn as you go), the gaps in your skill or knowledge could become obstacles for you.

Where do you begin? With a list of things you need to learn: your own reinvention curriculum.

When I started the health club, I already had a solid foundation in business from my time at Ratners. But jewellery and gyms are not the same. I needed to learn about membership structures, health and safety, gym equipment and lots more.

Whatever step you're taking, you can make the knowledge gap you need to traverse less daunting by literally writing a list of what you don't know.

This list will grow as you move ahead with your plans – the more you know, the more you know you don't know. Starting with a list means you can make progress in the most important areas. And just like any to do list, you're much more likely to succeed if you make the items bitesize.

If you're changing career, for example, you might need to retrain. That's a big item for the list; instead, you could start by learning about the different training options available and what you'll need to know to get onto the courses.

If you're moving to a different country, you might need to learn a new language. That's a massive undertaking (my patchy French can attest to this) that definitely warrants breaking down into chunks. You could first learn your options for learning – a class? Online course? Book and CD (if you're old-school)? Then you could learn the language itself in modules. You could also list things like reading books in your new language – I find children's story books are good practice.

I believe you can learn virtually any skill. We're all blank canvases when we're born, and given the right environment, we can develop in whatever direction we choose. The key is to figure out how you learn them – we all have different ways of acquiring skills.

What's your learning style?

I was never particularly academic; instead, I learned by watching people and rolling my sleeves up. I think that the success of any enterprise doesn't depend on sitting in an office looking at a balance sheet, moving numbers around. It depends on getting involved with the nuts and bolts of the business. If you want to do that, then you have to talk to the people who are at the sharp end of the business – people who are actually seeing the customers.

Graduates who leave university with a degree in business administration have a lot of knowledge that comes in very helpful when they start in a management position. But they don't really gain the skills they need to do the job until they've worked with the teams. I used to see this a lot when I would spend time with middle management at Ratners. (Lee Iacocca, who transformed the Ford Motor Company, wrote a brilliant autobiography in which he calls this method skip management. He would skip down a level and talk to the people who had more hands-on knowledge of the business.)

I liked to physically get stuck in. My plush corner office at Ratners wasn't piled high with papers like most other CEOs (it was the 80s, remember?), it was full of the jewellery we sold. I don't run companies like an accountant, I get down to basics: I familiarise myself with the products our customers choose between. I'm not a product expert, and I go to great lengths to hire the best buyers to make up for that, but I think every leader should learn about what they're selling.

I think by doing it this way round, it's better for the company in the long term. Accountants like to cut costs, so if you approach leadership from the profit and loss standpoint, you'll end up focusing on reducing overheads. But focus on what the customer wants, what the company is really about, and you'll focus on spending money and investing in the right places.

So my approach to learning in business is very physical: I use my body and my sense of touch. It's also social: I learn from and with other people. There are several different learning styles, all of which can help prepare you with the knowledge and skills you need for your reinvention. None are necessarily better than the others, but each of us will have a natural preference. Which is yours?

Aural: sound and music

Logical: mathematics

Physical: touch

Verbal: speech and writing

Visual: images and graphics

Each of these five approaches can either be done with others (social) or alone (solitary).

My physical social learning style meant the best way for me to grow at Ratners was to start at the bottom and work my way up. I'd worked in the shops on Oxford Street and in Richmond for years before taking a leadership position. I always felt that the people who didn't take that scenic route had a tremendous failing, because they never really understood the business.

That's not just the case for jewellery; I once spoke to a chef who said he'd rather promote someone who had worked in the kitchen at two o'clock in the morning and taken the rubbish out.

If you lean towards a certain learning approach, that doesn't mean you can't or shouldn't include others in your curriculum. As I've already mentioned, I listen to podcasts and audiobooks, and I read a lot. Books are a brilliant way to gain knowledge. If I have a hard copy, I like to take notes in the margin, mark the pages, read and re-read the useful parts.

Centuries ago, there was a good library at the heart of every Stoic philosopher's home. Cato, Cicero and Epictetus surrounded themselves with books. This habit has survived the ages; modern-day Stoic and finance expert Ramit Sethi has a 'book buying rule': 'If you're "thinking about" buying a book, just buy it. Don't waste five seconds debating. Even one idea makes it worth it.'

Whatever you do, if you pay attention and look for the lesson, you will always learn at least one thing.

Rob: cultivate curiosity

If you follow me, you'll probably know that I'm not a big fan of university degrees as a way to start a career. With the exception of practical professions like those you can find in medicine, I don't think three years of intense knowledge injection, from textbooks and often professors no longer practising, is the way to go. I know, I've been there. (I studied architecture… go figure.)

If you've passed university age, don't panic. Old dogs can learn new tricks. Just look at me! A lot of people think as they get older, it gets harder to learn. But that's not true. That's just the story we tell ourselves. In reality, you can often learn better when you're older. You have more experience and wisdom, more self-awareness and more control over your emotions.

The way we learn changes over time. As children, we soak up information like a sponge – if you've ever watched a toddler, you'll know they're little learning machines. Why? We're hungry for knowledge and skills, and we need them.

That thirst for learning fluctuates throughout our lives – through our teenage years, our brains change and turn us into monsters (or was that just me?). The ego takes over in our 20s and we get cocky. There's nothing you can teach me that I don't know!

I'm generalising and being really harsh here of course, but there's truth in it. I think it's not until we reach our thirties that we really start to take life's lessons on board. When I look at myself, I'm learning more than I ever have before, and I'm the oldest I've ever been (funny that). The more progressive and self-aware I've become, the more I've realised how little I know.

This is why I think it's far more effective to create your own educational program than it is to follow someone else's. And let me be really clear: if you want to succeed with your reinvention, you need to invest in your education. I've invested more than 1 million pounds in my personal development over the last 15 years, and that's what has helped me go from poor artist to multimillionaire.

A good education encompasses a few different elements. Having the right support system, with mentors and people you can learn from, will give you a strong foundation. On top of that, it's good to think about mindset development, knowledge acquisition, skill development and learning from people.

Mindset development

What really counts isn't age, it's something that age creates: a learning mindset. You have to believe that things are possible as you get older. Because they really are – just look at the people who are starting businesses at the age of 60 or becoming millionaires at 70. Colonel Sanders was in his 70s when he made his fortune by selling KFC. That was rare in the 1960s but far less surprising today!

When it comes to mindset, I think curiosity is the key to building yourself an education. Curiosity is wanting to learn from everyone, not overly looking down or up at anyone, staying inquisitive, wanting to learn everywhere you go, being fascinated about the world around you and always seeing new opportunities. Its opposite is stubbornness, closed mindedness, ego and arrogance, which will close your eyes to new information.

I write a lot about curiosity in the book I'm working on now, *Opportunity*. A curious mindset, wanting to learn from everyone and being intrigued and fascinated by everything is what will drive your education. You need to cultivate a sort of wonderment about people in the world. Let's be honest, the world and people are pretty amazing, so it shouldn't be hard to do. That is the greatest open mindset for learning and development, and that's what will fuel your reinvention, whatever area of your life it's in.

Knowledge acquisition

Finding information takes a fraction of the time it used to – thanks to fibre optic broadband, it's exchanged at the speed of light. If you know what knowledge gaps you need to close, you can figure out how to patch them up fast, with books, podcasts, documentaries, online courses and professional training, masterminds and mentorships, for example.

I learn so much from books and documentaries, and when I come across a topic or idea that I want to explore a bit more, I go in that direction and find more content. I like to go broad when researching, but then deep when focusing, implementing and scaling. There's so much content out there these days that you can even get a lot of this knowledge for free, or at a very low cost. If you decide to take that route, remember to do your due diligence: look carefully at the source of the information and decide whether it's trustworthy before you soak it up into your brain. Remember that free advice is often worth every penny.

Another way to acquire knowledge is to travel, literally and metaphorically. Get out of your home and go exploring – going to different countries and exploring different cultures will give you new knowledge that will feed into your broader perspective. By metaphorical travel, I mean get out of your familiar zone – learn about other professions, other markets, other hobbies.

Skill development

If you apply the knowledge you develop, the sky really is the limit – especially if you're working with digital technology and social media. I think it's absolute crap when people say today's tech is beyond the older generation. I see older people everywhere embracing technology, and it's keeping them young as learners.

When you've mastered (or even just got a bit familiar with) digital tools, you've got endless opportunities to learn and be successful online. It no longer takes a decade to be an overnight success; nine-year-old Ryan Kaji is already making more than $20 million a year with his Ryan's World franchise. Bastard. (Only kidding, I know I've said it before, but wow, that goes to show enthusiasm and JFDI can get you places! Note to his parents: I'll adopt him if you want rid of the young lad.)

Learning from people

It's so easy to learn from people you like and people you admire, you hang on their every word and usually what they say already lines up with your belief system. But with people you don't like (or think you don't like), you often judge them and put them away in a box so you don't need to pay attention to them.

I don't believe in that; I think it's a bad tactic. For one, you create that all-too-common echo chamber. Being open minded to learn from people you don't like, or people have different beliefs, is really powerful. It comes from curiosity. You don't agree with them, but you're curious to know why. Why do they believe what they believe? And what can you learn about their beliefs? It also comes from seeing all people on an equal, level playing field, and not putting people down or pedestalising them up.

For example, I'd consider myself more of a capitalist than a socialist, and recently I've tried to learn from people who are more socialist. Personally, I'd probably prefer Labour not to be voted in at this point, but there's someone in my company who votes Labour, and I'm fascinated to know why. By talking to him I'll get new insights. And then I can challenge my own thinking.

This is something investigative journalists like Louis Theroux are brilliant at. Theroux once said, 'I am genuinely a bit confused about the world, a little bit bumbling.' I think this is a fantastic state to be in – by acknowledging that he doesn't understand everything, he can ask questions, be curious and learn. (I've been trying and failing so far to get Louis on my Disruptive Entrepreneur podcast, so please let me know if you or anyone you know knows him and can connect us.)

Whether you look up to or disagree with them, other people are a really useful source of learning when it comes to your reinvention. And if you've got a good support system in place, all you have to do is start talking to the people around you – and listening really well.

Polymaths

If you're a big fan of reinvention, and you're willing to put in the time, learning will get you places – just ask the polymaths.

I want to address a contentious topic here. I hear a lot of people saying that the way to succeed in a venture, a career or in life is to focus: follow one course until successful. They say it's better to become an expert in one area, to specialise and become a leader in it rather than being a 'Jack of all trades, master of none'.

I completely disagree. I think this works for individual tasks, but over decades? No thanks. Most of the biggest names in business are generalists at the very least, and often polymaths. Besides, how boring would it be to do one thing for your whole life?!

If you're considering or working on your reinvention, you're more likely to be someone who has multiple interests, several skills or knowledge in various areas. And that's ok. In fact, it's more than ok; there's research that suggests people with 'too many interests' are more likely to be successful.

Polymaths – from the Greek for 'having learned much' – are people who have mastered more than one thing in their lives. Let's look at some of the great polymaths to understand what this can look like.

Leonardo da Vinci (1452-1519)

We'll start with arguably the most famous polymath of all time. Da Vinci was an accomplished artist, most well-known for painting the Mona Lisa. But he was also a gifted scientist, civil engineer and inventor, having designed everything from city infrastructure to flying machines that look an awful lot like helicopters. On top of that, he was an anatomist (rather gruesomely, he would dissect human cadavers to make his paintings more accurate), philosopher and prolific writer (often using mirror writing in his notebooks).

Benjamin Franklin (1707-1790)

One of the Founding Fathers of the United States, Benjamin Franklin was, in alphabetical order, a leading: civil activist, diplomat, Freemason, humourist, inventor, political philosopher, politician, postmaster, printer, scientist, statesman and writer. Note that I wrote 'leading' – he didn't just dabble in those things, he got great at them.

Marie Curie (1867-1934)

Polish-French scientist Marie Curie smashed the glass ceiling for women in science. She was a physicist and chemist who famously researched (and was ultimately killed by) radioactivity. She was a Nobel Prize winner, but she was no ordinary winner: she was the first woman to win, the first person (and still the only woman) to win twice, and the only person to win in two completely different scientific fields (physics and chemistry).

Hedy Lamarr (1914-2000)

Once dubbed the 'world's most beautiful woman', Hedy Lamarr had an extraordinary career and life. She was an Austrian-American actor and found fame when she starred in the controversial 1933 film *Ecstasy*. She went on to star in many movies until 1958 and was given a star on the Hollywood Walk of Fame in 1960. While she was acting, she also co-invented a radio guidance system for Allied torpedoes and helped improve aviation design during World War II. In 2014, she was posthumously inducted into the National Inventors Hall of Fame.

Elon Musk (1971-)

The Tesla founder is the epitome of the modern polymath. His interest in computers started when he was just ten, and within two years, he had taught himself computer programming. Fast-forward another 12 years and he had a bachelor's degree in physics and economics, going on to start (but, like so many entrepreneurs, not finish) a PhD in applied physics and materials science. His interests are so broad that his work as an engineer, entrepreneur, industrial designer and philanthropist is connected to the internet, green energy and, most recently, space exploration.

How to be a polymath

If your reinvention is connected to your field of study, work or hobby, you can think of it as your path to becoming a polymath. Going in a new direction will open all sorts of opportunities for you, by creating a niche you can dominate.

You can use all the tools and tactics we've been sharing in this book to reinvent yourself and become a polymath. In particular:

1. Choose your new field to master. If you're feeling ambitious, why not choose two? Think about spanning left and right brain subjects – if your first area of expertise is something analytical, science or engineering-based, go for something creative. This is a well-known combination among polymaths and has been shown to be a clear path to success by sparking innovation.

2. Set a goal and specific targets. Visualise, write yourself a letter, do everything you can to make achieving the goal feel inevitable.

3. JFDI. Start now, get perfect later, as Rob says.

4. Create a curriculum. What do you need to know, learn and develop to master this new thing? Put together a program of books, events, documentaries, courses and mentors.

5. Practise, fail, try again. This cycle is what will help you become a master – and a polymath.

If we accept the idea that it takes 10,000 hours to become an expert at something, that's five years of practising 40 hours a week, with a couple of weeks' holiday a year. A serious investment. But you don't need to be the best at something to excel at it; while you will need to invest time and effort in honing your new skills, it doesn't have to mean five solid years of hard work.

This is truer than ever today, given the accessibility of knowledge and training materials. And there are examples everywhere of people who became experts in a flash. Twelve-year-old Adilyn Malcolm became a dubstep dance master in months, learning from YouTube videos. Thirteen-year-old Michael Sayman learned to code on Google and ended up developing a top-100 app.

So instead of looking at becoming a polymath as an impossibly difficult, drawn out process, just jump in and kick off your reinvention. You're already headed in the right direction!

CHAPTER 11
Disrupt Yourself

When news reports about the Coronavirus first started appearing, like most of the people I know, I took it all with a pinch of salt. In the last decade we'd seen warnings of several terrifying diseases that could ravage the global population, from bird flu to Ebola virus. Two of those warnings had been about different Coronaviruses too – SARS and MERS – and it blew over both times.

But as with any big warning, I kept it in my mind and rolled the risks around with my businesses. That's what you do when you've got a strategic brain – I can't help it. Wherever I look I see potential futures, and if one looks plausible enough, it runs through my head as a scenario.

The clearer and more damning the press reports got, the more seriously I took the virus on board as a risk. Finally, when the pandemic was declared and the lockdown came into effect, the situation changed for real. Events were cancelled, and with them, my speaking engagements. Very quickly, my calendar emptied. I was scheduling like mad to keep myself busy.

Then the effects rippled out to the jewellery business: Gerald Online took a nosedive in sales, just like every other retailer. Because when your entire future is at stake, the last thing you're thinking about is buying a necklace. And since weddings were cancelled everywhere, that side of the market had crashed hard.

I've been in the jewellery business long enough to be more than familiar with its seasonality – it's the second most seasonal product group next to fireworks. If you look at a graph of jewellery sales of any company, you'll see that jewellery sells at Christmas; sales during the rest of the year pale in comparison.

Because of this, we've always operated Gerald Online in a way that we could easily take it offline if that made sense from an overheads perspective, then bring it back for the Christmas rush. When the pandemic hit, it hit us hard, so we decided to take it offline. It means we can minimise costs while there's no money coming in and be ready to restart as soon as it makes sense again.

It wasn't something we were happy about doing, of course, but it was necessary. We've done brilliantly with Gerald Online – when we started in 2002, right after the dotcom bubble burst, everyone said there was no future in online sales. But we had a phenomenal period early on and we were bringing in £25 million a year. In partnership with my Indian factory, we now do a lot of wholesale, supplying Amazon and shopping channels. But of course, all that has slowed too.

Pausing the company was an act of disruption on our part. We changed what we were doing – and did something differently to the rest of the industry. When you embrace change and take action to move with it, what you're effectively doing is disrupting yourself.

Almost all successful businesses look at an industry and then turn it upside-down. They break all the rules, and approach business in a completely different way. Look at the hotel industry for example. Traditionally, you need nice premises, a smartly dressed person on the door and fluffy white bathrobes hanging next to heated mirrors. Then came along companies like Travelodge, seeing the change coming in travel and hospitality, and opened up the budget market. And now Airbnb is the world's biggest accommodation company… and it owns no hotels.

We know the examples – Uber disrupted transport, becoming the biggest taxi company without owning a single cab, and Lyft did the same in the US; Stashbee is disrupting storage, Spotahome is disrupting lettings and Hubble is taking hot-desking to the next level. People forget that Facebook is a media outlet, just like a newspaper or a magazine. They publish, and brilliantly, they don't employ any journalists – we do it for them. And we read it too. There are loads more examples: Instagram, the world's most valuable photo company, doesn't sell cameras; Bitcoin has no cash; Skype owns no telecom infrastructure. These are all companies that saw the shift to the sharing economy and jumped in at the right time.

When you're disrupting, you're wrecking. I did that in the jewellery business when I was running Ratners: it had always been about prestige, and I threw that in the bin. I've done it in other industries outside of my expertise too – if you have your eyes and your mind open to change, you can take opportunities you wouldn't even imagine existed.

As the COVID-19 pandemic forced us into a new reality, disruption suddenly became widespread. This brought with it a massive amount of destruction – as we've seen, there have been plenty of corporate casualties. But it also sparked innovation, which is one of the most satisfying and exciting results of disruption.

Disruptive desserts

One of my favourite examples is Gü – makers of delicious posh desserts. I mentioned them back in chapter 6 on getting started, because they tested the market really well by perfecting their packaging before they began production.

We're all used to seeing premium desserts on the shelves now, but that wasn't always the case. Looking back, the first in the UK to produce them was Marks & Spencer, and they did well with their range. Supermarkets like Tesco and Sainsbury's had desserts, but they weren't marketed as exclusive. In walked two men with a beautifully packaged, expensive-looking product that was appealing, foreign (or so it seemed) and delicious. Gü (which, thanks to the umlaut, appeared to be Belgian but was actually producing desserts in Crewe) took the market by storm. This was down to the unlikely but brilliant pairing of a no-frills and difficult but smart Israeli and a quintessential, suited-and-booted Englishman with a gift for sales.

They had built Gü from scratch, and their success was in the marketing. They saw a change in the market, and rather than going with the status quo, they pushed it and disrupted desserts. From the mystique surrounding the name to the packaging that's nice enough to hang onto, they hit the jackpot.

A few years after Gü appeared on the scene, I was doing a speech for the person who supplies most of the eggs to the UK's supermarkets, £400 million worth of eggs. He had reached a 50 percent monopoly in the supply of eggs, so he had to diversify. I introduced him to Gü; I could see the synergy with that deal – a lot of eggs go into desserts. He bought the business and made a huge amount of money, taking it global. He hadn't been in the dessert business, but he had his eyes and mind open to change, and he was willing to take a risk.

The beauty of life is its unpredictability. Nobody can predict the future, and you should embrace that. Don't let yourself get long in the tooth and say, 'I've always done it this way, and this is what I've always believed.' Things are constantly changing, and you need to be changing with them. Today's world is different to yesterday's, and tomorrow's will be different still. Isn't that exciting?

One more thing...

I think disruption is exciting, but you don't have to go in blindfolded and trip yourself up. When I give my speeches, I know I've refined them to the point where I can trust the jokes will land and not offend too much, that I'm giving people the right amount of detail and that I'm being entertaining enough. I know that because I've done the same speech thousands of times. The situation is already stressful enough, without what I'm saying being an unknown.

It's the same in business. When you start your new venture, you want to be pretty certain that you're going to be successful. If you know that, you'll deliver. I deliver my speech well, because I'm confident it's good. If you have confidence in your venture, you'll follow through and succeed.

That's what I do: I forensically examine a situation before jumping in, so I'm certain it will work. I call this the Columbo method.

Have you ever seen the TV program Columbo? The star of the show is a trench coat-clad detective whose catchphrase is 'one more thing…' – he makes people think he believes them, and he lets them talk themselves into a hole. He watches, listens, makes connections and then bam, shoots them with the truth.

I was always impressed by how he did that. He really believed nothing until it was proven, and he would get the facts for himself. Columbo would have made a brilliant CEO by doing things his way and checking everything, going into the detail. I've always tried to channel him in what I do, which is a lot of the reason I have this forensic approach.

There isn't an easy fix in business, you have to actually know your products. I mean really know them. You have to be an expert in your field, and that takes time. That time investment is totally worth it – not only will it put you above the competition, if they don't make that same investment, it could sink them even lower.

When I was running Ratners, we had the chance to acquire the huge chain H. Samuel for this exact reason. The people running it had decided it was time for a redesign. Instead of applying expert advice, they called in a design company that knew nothing about the jewellery business and gave them free reign in all their stores. At the time, in the late 1980s, it was fashionable for retail to be stylish – Topshop had just been redesigned, and H. Samuel wanted in on the trend.

The design company made the shops look fabulous. They were sparkly and sleek and beautiful. But they were an absolute flop – the design was totally uncommercial for the locations H. Samuel operated in. They were mid- to down-market, they weren't Tiffany's. Everything was wrong, right down to the colour scheme. The thing that most surprised me was the way the products were displayed.

There's a rule of 42 in the jewellery business: we always display diamond rings 42 inches from the ground. This is absolutely paramount – I learned it from my father, and it was passed down to him too. There's a simple reason for this: the average woman in the UK is five feet and four inches tall, and the trajectory of her eye falls at 42 inches from the ground. That's where you want to put the shiny rings.

There are other fundamental rules, and the new design was smashing them all – not in a good way. I visited one of the H. Samuel shops in Northern Ireland before Christmas one year, and they had all the lovely new branding, the colours, and so on. As I walked into the shop at nine in the morning, I noticed immediately that they had displayed all the watches on the top shelves, with their dials facing upward. You couldn't see the at all, it was unbelievable.

The rest of the shop was just as bad. Everything was displayed at the wrong height and it was all badly lit. You have to place items of jewellery, which are small, in just the right position, with perfect halogen lighting that makes them sparkle; this hadn't even been considered. The designers didn't understand the basics. To make things worse, they had covered the windows, which was really the shop's calling card, especially in pre-internet days, with icicle stickers, so you could hardly see anything. I spoke to the manager, who had been in the trade for 25 years after joining as an apprentice; they hadn't even consulted him. He thought it was a complete and utter joke.

On the face of it, this shop wasn't in great shape, but I'd done my homework. I knew what their sales were before I even considered the acquisition. That's not an easy thing to find out, but I Columboed it.

When I was considering taking over a store or a chain, I would check in with local estate agents first, and they'd invariably tell me it was a great town, great prospects and so on. But when you're Columbo, you can't take their word for it. You need proof. So I used to call shops on the phone to get their sales figures. I used to say 'it's head office here. We've got a query on your figures: you got 12,000 last week,' and they'd say, indignantly, 'no, no, we didn't take 12,000, we took 18,200'. Then I'd think, yeah, I'll go into that town. It's worth it.

That's the acid test. Never mind about all the speculation, or looking at figures and taking a guesstimate as to whether it's going to work, or going on the word of advisors. People have got hidden agendas – they will advise you based on what they want the outcome to be. You need real information about what's going on if you want to make good decisions.

I also channelled Columbo to dig into dips in our own figures. If a shop had had a bad week, I would call a shop run by another company in the area to compare figures; I could see pretty quickly if it was location-related or specific to one of our branches, in which case I'd need to speak to the manager.

That same Christmas I visited Northern Ireland, I did my Columbo thing with the then Department of Trade and Industry (DTI), which collates retail sales figures for the entire industry. I knew the trick worked with anyone if you spoke with authority, so I called a representative there, told her I was from head office (which isn't a lie, I just wasn't from that head office), and she handed over the figures for H. Samuel for the entire Christmas period.

They were absolutely diabolical, which I knew they would be. And we'd had a phenomenal Christmas, thanks mainly to our new strategy. I made a bid to buy the company because I knew that they'd be on their knees, and I knew the problem could be fixed. I was already armed with information their shareholders didn't yet have; I was in a strong position.

But it wasn't going to be easy; it was a very difficult business to acquire. Firstly, they owned half of their 450 properties outright. Imagine that – they didn't have to pay rent on half their locations. (And still they were doing badly…!) And the locations were sensational and big. Plus they had a great name: H. Samuel had been going since 1883 and had been huge in the 50s and 60s. It was the crown jewel of the UK market, and everyone wanted it.

The biggest obstacle was the directors: they owned over 50 percent of the business, so they could stick two fingers up to anybody.

Out came Columbo again. I charmed the chairman. I took him to eat, I watched as he drank a bottle of wine (while I drank water), and I listened to his stories. I let him carry on about how fantastic he was and how he had achieved such amazing success. I made him feel like I thought he was the bees' knees, and that he would be an outstanding chairman of an even bigger company.

This went on for quite a while. Eventually, he said, 'yes, Gerald, I'll allow you to work for me as a chairman', and we shook hands and merged the companies. Three months later, I fired him. We converted all the H. Samuel shops to the Ratners layout, and within a year, we had increased profits from £3 million to £60 million.

For me, it wasn't all about the success of the company; I was exercising my mind, and it felt great.

Keep your eyes open and your brain switched on

The Columbo approach isn't for everyone – if you like doing things by the book, it won't be a good solution. But there are fundamental elements to it that are absolutely necessary in business, and in many other areas of life, especially if you're making a big change, or reinventing.

It's about having your eyes open, being flexible and collecting the information you need in order to make the right move. That's the forensic element – you need to see the whole story before you can write the next chapter.

That forensic approach is the reason we were successful across the Atlantic – and to this day, Ratners (now Signet Jewelers) is the only British retailer in the business that has succeeded in conquering the American market.

One thing the forensic approach does is stop you from getting arrogant. You rely on facts, on information, not on ego. That's where most other companies fell foul when trying to break America – they were arrogant and thought they could just replicate the approach that had earned them success in the UK. But that's not how it works.

I learned this the hard way, in the Netherlands. Before Ratners crossed the Atlantic, I decided to export our winning formula across the North Sea. We went over there, found a great opportunity and acquired a business. It didn't take long to realise we'd made a huge mistake. In fact, Christmas seems to be the blacklight that shows you failure in the jewellery industry.

The shop had been doing pretty well, and we were heading towards the festive season, so I was excited about the enormous boost in sales we were expecting to see. That's how it works in this business – you tend to make more over Christmas than you do the rest of the year. So imagine my surprise, then shock, then concern, then oh-shit-what-have-we-done when the sales didn't budge in December.

Here's the thing. In England, sales skyrocket in December because everyone exchanges Christmas presents. What I'd failed to realise is that in Holland, people don't exchange Christmas presents. That's not a thing. And we only discovered that after Christmas.

There were other things we hadn't counted on too. The Netherlands is a quality-driven, expensive market, and when people invest in jewellery, they take their time over it. The Dutch don't throw their money around, and they don't buy cheap jewellery as Christmas presents. The Ratners approach was an epic fail there.

The lesson is that everything about Holland was different. Just like everything about France is different. And America. If you want to get it right, you need local knowledge, local experience. We were effectively acting like the arrogant arseholes who went in and redesigned the Londonderry H. Samuels without asking the manager who had a quarter of a century of experience there.

Needless to say, I didn't make that same mistake twice.

I'd watched with interest as company after company took the leap into the American market and hobbled back, wounded and defeated. Tesco spent a year running a mock-up shop there before they accepted it had flopped. Marks & Spencer failed out there, despite spending a fortune on advisors, management consultants and market researchers. They overdid it on the research without even getting to the raw truth. They weren't Columbo.

I was, and that gave us a big advantage. We ditched the arrogance that had sunk us in the Netherlands, and we went in there with our eyes and minds open. America is a totally different market. We speak the same language, but that's pretty much where the similarity ends.

Ratners was hitting the jackpot down-market in the UK, but that would been a big mistake for America; at that time, everyone in the States was buying on credit. And they were discerning: customers would go into jewellery stores with a gem scope. They'd think you were barmy if you pulled one of those out in England. These are things you have to respect – you can't change the market, but you can change yourself. Approaching a new market calls for reinvention.

So, it was Columbo time again. The great thing about this in America is that it's not as cloak-and-dagger as it seems in the UK; people are much more open with information across the pond. It's something that's ingrained in the culture there – think about courtroom reports and police press conferences. When something happens in the US, it's on TV for everyone to see; in the UK, it's all kept under wraps.

When I went to the States, I went directly to the malls, where the jewellery stores were. I met with all the mall owners, who were happy to volunteer information, because it was in their interest to see the companies under their roofs succeed. They would give me the figures, tell me which stores were making the most money. The more I investigated, the more it became clear that one company was making more money than the others: Sterling.

Sterling had 125 shops, and they wanted $125 million for the lot. There was another chain up for grabs at the time, with 180 shops for $16 million. In other words, Sterling was almost ten times more expensive than the other chain. We went to the Sterling head office, met with the CEO, and within 24 hours, we had bought the business.

Everyone said I was mad because I chose the expensive one, and I did it on the basis of my Columbo-style investigation. After spending time with the people in the shops, I knew that they had the management and the skills, and after talking to the mall owners, I knew they were taking a lot of money.

After the deal went through and the news of the acquisition had hit the headlines, I remember sitting outside one of the shops. This old homeless guy came up to me and said, 'Did you know that some idiot from England paid a million dollars for this store?' I didn't care. I knew that this was the beginning of something huge, and I was right: while I was at Ratners, we took that chain to 1,250, and today it's a chain of over 3,500 shops.

Rob: The Disruptive Entrepreneur

Gerald's idea of disruption in business is measured, considered, strategic. It goes against what you might think about the notion of disruption at first glance. In our daily vocabulary, it's often used as a negative – kids who are disruptive in class, disruption to the train times, a news bulletin that disrupts EastEnders. But in business, it's positive, and it's far from chaotic.

In my podcast, I ask my guests what they think the word 'disruptive' means. There's a collection of quotes in the introduction to each episode, with all sorts of entrepreneurs and leaders in different fields sharing their thoughts: it's finding a new way, shaking things up, innovating.

Now, since I own the trademark for Disruptive Entrepreneur™, I suppose I'd better have something to say about it too.

I do (of course ;)).

The first point I want to make is that you don't have to be Uber to be disruptive; life and business and disruption and challenging the status quo all exist very happily outside of the big unicorns. Disruption is not measured in quarterly P&L sheets; you can be hugely disruptive in a very small niche and make little to no financial impact. You can also be disruptive socially or culturally and change the world without making any business impact.

Being the Disruptive Entrepreneur, I get the occasional comment or complaint that the phrase is overused, outdated, tired, misused and so on. To be honest, I don't care. I've never been bothered if people are tired of a phrase; if it's relevant (and I sincerely hope it stays that way in this case) and it's useful, let's use it!

To me, disruptive entrepreneurs are people who think differently about a problem in order to provide a new solution. They take risks and do the opposite of the masses. Instead of copying, they create. They hybridise experience from different industries, fusing and merging apparently unrelated ideas to create something new, like Rage Against the Machine did with rock, metal and hip hop. They ensure constant improvement: evolution or revolution.

Disrupt or die

It's not enough to be disruptive for the sake of it, or just change slowly or when something external forces you to change. You have to disrupt yourself. Even at the best of times, you have to pre-empt change and keep yourself on your toes. In fact, I'd argue the best time to disrupt yourself is when things are going well, before it's too late. You know how it feels when you've been sitting on the sofa for so long that your body has pushed itself into a perfectly comfortable mould and it's hard to get up? That's what happens when you sit still for too long in business. And if you get that stuck in position, a remote control isn't going to help.

If things stay the same, they fall behind. As Ray Croc said: 'If you're green you grow, if you're ripe you rot'. Things grow or the decay. And if you've reached the point where change is pushing you from the outside, it might be too late to change from the inside.

You need to shake things up before the cracks start to appear. This doesn't have to be huge or risky, small, frequent steps will make just as much difference. Just change little and often, keep moving forward. Keep testing, tweaking, reviewing and repeating.

I believe disrupting yourself means challenging your thinking, challenging your strategies, looking at how you need to protect yourself from downside risk. Here's a helpful exercise: ask yourself some questions and let your imagination run wild.

1. Imagine you are your competitor. How would you try and take you out?

2. What flaws would you pick on if you were attacking you?

3. You're you again. How could you disrupt yourself now to pre-empt the strike?

These little movements, the skips you make as your competitor dances around you with gloves up, are the hallmarks of continuous disruption. You end up reinventing yourself over and over, in slow motion. It's more like an evolution than a reinvention. It's lower risk, it's easier, it's slower. And even better is that your competition don't stand a chance. Even if they do copy you, which they will because the best are always copied, they'll be too slow and too far behind you.

Disrupting your reinvention

You might need to make a bigger, more dramatic change than that – a revolutionary reinvention. Revolution rather than evolution, forced by tough or external circumstances. And what if the disruption you need to make is to your reinvention? It might not be the straight path you're envisioning; in fact, success and results and change rarely are linear, they are usually messy, and you may need to make adjustments while you're on your journey.

Disruption is a form of change, and the key to embracing it is to be open.

1. Write flexibility into your plan. Having a rigid plan in place for your reinvention might help you implement it, but it could slip you up if you need to adjust. How can you inject some flexibility into your plan, to allow for changes and to make your reinvention a bit more malleable? It's not a failure if you change plan, it's just a step closer to your success or your goal. Or maybe a better goal is actually the end goal.

2. Be inquisitive. We've seen why it's important to listen actively and be curious; apply that to disruption and you'll be better able to spot risks and opportunities that could force changes. Keep asking questions. Stay humble.

3. Keep your eyes open. Like Gerald says, be Colombo.

4. Work on your confidence. Believe in your ability to reach your goal, no matter what shifts and obstacles you come across.

Words of wisdom from some of the greats

I have interviewed many amazing people on my Disruptive Entrepreneur Podcast, and as I mentioned, I ask them what the word 'disruption' means to them. Here are some of their answers, to inspire you to be more disruptive as you reinvent yourself.

Michael Gerber (entrepreneur and author): 'It means going beyond the ordinary, going beyond the status quo, being the chief aggravator, pissing everyone off, not thinking in a conventional way, not just sort of following the herd.'

Theo Paphitis (retail tycoon and Dragon): 'Not following the norm, moving people or things away from the norm and doing things differently. And that is more important today than any time in history.'

Jeff Hoffman (billionaire entrepreneur): 'Not accepting things the way it's always been done, assuming just because "experts" before you did it that way, that it makes it the right way. Don't accept the rules, don't assume the people who wrote the books were smarter than you, leave open the possibility there might be a better way to do this and give it a shot.'

Jack Cowin (billionaire fast-food mogul): 'Being prepared to accept change is a constant, nothing will ever remain the same – we are living in a world today where change is more rapid than ever.'

Robin Sharma (author): 'To get the results which only 5 percent have, you have to be willing to do what 95 percent of the population isn't willing to do. And if you do the things very few do, you get rewards very people are going to get.'

Kanye West

As far as celebrities go, Kanye West has to be among the most disruptive. The rapper-turned-entrepreneur-turned-fashion-designer-turned-[gulp]-politician has done much worse on stage than I ever did. He's hugely controversial, and he's mastered reinvention quite unlike anyone else.

Kanye the producer

West started showing interest in music and poetry at a young age, and as a teenager he was already recording. He started as a producer in the mid-90s, working with several different artists before he was signed to management production company Hip Hop Since 1978. Two years later, he was producing for Roc-A-Fella Records, working with Jay-Z, Cam'ron, Ludacris and Janet Jackson, among others.

Kanye the rapper

He was becoming a renowned producer, but West really wanted to perform. Reluctantly, Roc-A-Fella Records signed him in 2002, releasing his debut record the following year. It was inspired by a car accident he had, in which he damaged his jaw and the other driver broke both his legs. He recorded the first single, called 'Through the Wire', with his jaw wired shut.

Kanye the controversial public speaker

I must admit, I have some empathy for him on this front, although it does appear that he can't learn from his mistakes. West was a featured speaker during a benefit concert for Hurricane Katrina in 2005. When it was his turn to speak, he went off-piste and announced: 'George Bush doesn't care about black people.' As you can imagine, that didn't go down well with the President. In 2009, he famously jumped on stage and took Taylor Swift's mic during her acceptance speech at the VMAs, telling everyone that Beyoncé had deserved the win. It was a shocker, but it didn't seem to do him much harm – Billboard named him the Top Male Artist of 2009.

Kanye the actor

At the height of her fame as a reality TV celebrity, Kim Kardashian welcomed Kanye into their family – and their hit TV show – in 2013, when they announced the birth of their first child, North West. He has also appeared in various TV shows and films, including *Entourage* and *The Cleveland Show*. He premiered a short film he directed at Cannes in 2012, and in 2018, he announced he was setting up the film production company Half Beast LLC.

Kanye the fashion designer

West released his first clothing line in 2005 and collaborated with Nike on a shoe in 2009. He launched a fashion line with Adidas, called Yeezy Season 1, in 2013. Over the years, he has collaborated with various designers and has launched fashion lines for women and children.

Kanye the philosopher

In a surprising left field move, West announced he was working on a philosophy book in 2018 called *Break the Simulation*. He was publishing it in real time on Twitter. Reviews of the tweets said the content was more like life coaching than philosophy.

Kanye the Christian musician

In 2019, West started the Sunday Service Choir – a gospel group that performs every Sunday. They did an additional performance on Friday 27 September 2019, when West released a Christian hip hop album called 'Jesus is King'.

Kanye the entrepreneur

West's first foray into the business side of music was in 2004, when he founded GOOD Music. He ran a couple of fast food restaurants some years later, then in 2012, he launched a creative content company called DONDA. He is quoted as having said at the time, the company would 'pick up where Steve Jobs left off'. He is also involved in the artist-owned music streaming platform Tidal.

Kanye the politician

Well, things couldn't get stranger than they have been in the White House... could they? For several years, there have been rumours – often started by West – that he planned to run for President. His support for Trump and the Republicans has swayed, though he has told reporters that he intended to vote for Trump. With his campaign slogan #2020Vision, only West knows what his intentions were in the race to the White House.

CHAPTER 12
Look for the Silver Lining

Bear looked at me with expectation in his eyes as I turned the sausages on the barbecue and took a sip of my beer. I always marvel at how effortlessly he displays the traits I have to try so hard to maintain – like patience. Sausages always take far longer than you expect on a barbecue, and he didn't bark once.

In the middle of the pandemic, we had an uncommonly good summer, weather-wise. At the end of July, temperatures hit 30 degrees Celsius here in England. It was glorious: pins out, sunglasses on, I got outside and basked in the sunshine, with Bear curled up next to me.

There's something about being slowly toasted by the sun that puts life into perspective for me. Maybe it's the reminder that I'm a tiny human in a vast solar system, or maybe it's just the blast of vitamin D boosting my energy levels and helping me think clearly.

We had weeks of solid sunshine and tropical temperatures, and with them came lots of boats, barbecues and Bear. It was an extended holiday, really. Sure, we were all in lockdown, but we could get out for a walk and there were no restrictions on sitting in the garden with a glass of something cold. And for those of us working from home, we could do worse than a deckchair and a laptop.

This doesn't seem overly optimistic or positive to me; I was just looking at the reality of the situation for what it is, and being grateful for my life. But listening to everyone moaning about it, you'd think I had come straight from the cast of *The Sound of Music*.

We're hardwired to talk about the weather – it's the standard British conversation opener. I think the fact that it's so average most of the time makes people completely intolerant of the extremes. The moment it gets a bit too hot, cold, windy or rainy, it's all people talk about. The summer of 2020 was no different – we were experiencing weather that people pay thousands of pounds to visit once a year, and all they could do was moan about how much they were sweating.

Of course, this was against the backdrop of a traumatic experience. The COVID-19 pandemic affected every one of us, to varying degrees. Thousands of people lost their lives, or their loved ones. Millions lost their jobs, their income, their stability. People lost businesses, from high street giants to one-person lifestyle companies. It's the biggest, hardest thing we've had to collectively deal with since World War II.

But even in the midst of the War, people facing disaster and devastation kept their spirits up, made a cup of tea, kept calm and carried on. We're famous for our Blitz spirit.

In the middle of the lockdown, I listened to a program on BBC Radio 5 in which several entrepreneurs were interviewed about missing out on Coronavirus compensation. The government scheme to support small businesses was set up in a way that meant about 2 million people fell through the cracks and didn't get a penny of support. They were in tears on the phone, they were complaining about how unfair life is.

Well, life is unfair. The world doesn't owe us, it's not obliged to arrange things in a way that makes each of us ok. The pandemic and lockdown experience was at the extreme end, but unfairness and unexpected challenges are simply the nature of the beast of being in business. Things like this do happen.

I have a huge amount of empathy, especially for people who have started a business in the last year or two. I know how it feels to lose everything. But I also know that lying down and focusing on how awful everything is will not help you. In the short term, it'll make you feel worse; in the long term, it will limit your success.

This is where reinvention is quite literally a life saver. There was one caller on that Radio 5 program who was very successful – he ran a business servicing boats. When the lockdown hit, he suddenly had no turnover. What did he do? He reinvented himself, and fast. He started delivering food. He was earning a third of what he did before the pandemic, but he was bringing in money to pay the bills.

If you think about it, what is the point of getting sympathy from people? What's it going to get you aside from reinforcing your negative feelings? I could have moaned and felt sorry for myself, just like those callers: conference speaking is pretty high up on the list of things that have been affected the worst, and it's likely to be the last thing to get back up to speed. But there's no use in me holding on to how unfair it all is, it's much better to pivot, figure out what I can do.

I've written this book. I've done podcast interviews. I'm doing webinars. Ok, I'm getting a fraction of what I would for an in-person speech, but it's something.

I have the advantage of experience, of course. In the 50 years I've been in business, there have been a lot of disasters. We've had the three-day week, purchase tax hyped up to 55 percent, we've had the gold collapse, the banking crisis, the dotcom crash, and several recessions.

This is the private sector. There are big rewards, but also huge dangers. When the proverbial hits the fan, you need enough resilience to keep going. If that means you're stacking shelves for a while, so be it. The worst thing you can do is sit there and complain about your situation. I know, I did it for seven years, and it nearly killed me.

I think this realisation that wallowing doesn't pay is what has made me so much more optimistic. And it becomes easier to be optimistic when you realise that the old adage is true: every cloud really does have a silver lining.

Finding the silver lining

Have you ever put on a pair of night vision goggles? It's amazing, it's like you can suddenly see a hidden world, one that had been cloaked in darkness. It's mysterious and green, and even if you're looking at a familiar scene, it seems different. You notice new things, you see it all from a new perspective.

I think finding the silver lining is a bit like putting on night vision goggles. Contrary to the metaphor, it's rarely as shiny and visible as you expect – it's not right there, for everyone to see. You have to look for it. And having goggles helps. Not night vision ones, but optimism ones.

When you wallow, you take those glasses off and all you see is darkness. It's a cycle, and you have to break it. You'll only find the silver lining if you look at your situation with optimism, and when you do find it, you'll become even more optimistic. I believe that optimism is a decision, not an inherent character trait. You can be grumpy and still be optimistic.

There are lots of things you can do to put these optimism goggles on. Two things I think work well together are to get out and slow down.

I spent years behind closed doors, pickling in my own sadness. The longer I stayed there, isolated from the outside world, the harder it got to open the door and walk outside. I used the smell analogy earlier in this book – you don't notice the bad smell when you've been in the room all along. In order to notice the smell, you need to get outside.

This works whatever situation you're in – whether you're at a low point, in a rut or on top of your game. You need fresh air – literally and metaphorically. So put your phone and laptop away, open the front door and walk outside. Change your surroundings, get into nature, talk to people in real life. Doing this changes the angle of the light that's illuminating your situation, and it lets you see things differently.

Slowing down purposefully helps too. When I was at Ratners, I was constantly moving at the speed of light. I never used to travel by train because it wasn't fast enough; I flew everywhere. I even drove down the hard shoulder on a few occasions to get past traffic (I know, I know).

Today, I'm not in such a rush – I enjoy a train journey. I'm more relaxed and I can switch off, which I could never do before. This is really helpful, because it means I can see more of what's happening right now. If you're rushing, moving fast, you miss things. You don't register people, events, beautiful landscapes, even your own emotions. By slowing down, you can see more of the real picture, which makes it easier to see the upside too.

The silver linings of The Speech

When people ask me whether I'm glad that I said what I said in The Speech, I always wonder what on earth they're thinking. That's a ridiculously stupid question. Of course I'm not glad I said it, it was a huge mistake. Just because I found the silver linings and reinvented myself, doesn't mean I don't regret it.

Would I have still been running Ratners if I hadn't made that speech? I don't see why not. I was running it pretty well until then. Do I miss it? Probably, yes. But if I had stayed, I would have been doing exactly the same thing today. Instead, I've had a rich and varied life, working in health, public speaking and jewellery, not to mention having the time and freedom to enjoy my life.

I lost everything in what was possibly the biggest blunder of all time. But paradoxically, I'm happier than I was when I was at the top of my business game. Here are some of the silver linings I found.

Appreciation

I've found that having a bit less than I need makes me appreciate things more. Now, I'm not glamorising poverty, and I would never suggest putting yourself in financial hardship to get a bit of perspective. But looking at the upside, being skint definitely made me more grateful for what I had.

I had to move out of Mayfair when I lost everything, away from my £20 million (in today's money) house. My life is definitely different now. I don't have the flash house, the helicopter rides, the Concorde flights, the boats – all the things I completely failed to appreciate at the height of my wealth. But you know what I do have? A garden that I love. Art I enjoy. Holidays I relax on.

Having all of that money is no good to you, unless you get your head sorted out and get some perspective in life. I'm not a billionaire, but I'm comfortable. And I'm happy, without having to chase more and more money, because I appreciate what I have.

Balance

I've found more balance in my life. If you're constantly switched on in business, it's liable to take over your life. It was so absorbing for me, so engrossing and exciting, that going home felt mundane in comparison. If I'm honest, it was hard to sit down at the table and engage in conversation when my head was still spinning. Even at dinner parties, I wasn't interested in hearing what other people had to say. I had become self-obsessed and completely out of balance.

Paul Tsongas, a US Senator, is quoted as saying: 'Nobody on his deathbed ever said "I wish I had spent more time at the office".' *Financial Times* columnist Lucy Kellaway called this 'sentimental pap' and pointed out that it's almost certainly untrue, because there's no way we could know. But I can't imagine anyone lamenting their failure to log more work hours. It seems mad to me.

Balance is one of the best things to have come out of my downfall. I don't work as hard as I used to work running a public company. And I think I'm better for it. I still work hard, but I prioritise time with the people who matter, and give myself the space to relax and enjoy life.

Bear

I had a dog when I was running Ratners, but I hardly noticed. I didn't walk it, and I didn't really care. I honestly had no idea what I was missing.

That dog has long since passed away, and today, our 12-year-old dog Bear is part of the family. I walk him every day, and it's one of the greatest pleasures in my life.

Family

When you lose all your money, you stop worrying about yourself and instead worry about your family. Losing it all made me less selfish, despite the wallowing. I became a much better father and a better husband – a family man.

I remember being particularly concerned about my eldest daughter. Being at home meant I could support her in a positive step in her life. One day, when she was 18, she said: 'As you've lost your job and won't be wearing your suit and tie any more, can I have all your ties?' I was perplexed, but I humoured her. It turns out she had a plan to sell them. They were designer ties – Hermès, Gucci, Valentino – and she didn't get much for them, but that income helped her fend for herself. She has since worked her way up from there, and she's now a top television producer.

There were many moments like that with my kids. When I lost my job, someone pointed out that I'd be able to go to plays and functions that I'd been too busy to attend before. My busy job had almost been an excuse; it's not just about having the time for family, it's your state of mind when you're at home. When I had the freedom to spend time with my family, I realised what I had been missing out on. You get a lot out of it, just as your kids do, by making an effort.

Running a large public company puts a strain on your relationship too. I had gone through one marriage because of my adrenaline addiction, and it was affecting my marriage to Moira. She suffered not only because I lost the money, but because of my behaviour. But now our marriage is in a much stronger place: I admire her and respect her so much. She had every reason to leave, but instead, she stayed, supported me, and gave me the kick I needed to get back to life. It has brought us closer together, and I appreciate her every day.

Health

I'm much healthier now than I was when I was running Ratners, but to me, that's not the best thing about getting fit. The best thing was discovering cycling.

To me, cycling is so much more than exercise. I cycle for a couple of hours in the morning, and it puts me in the right frame of mind for the day. I get my best ideas out there, because my mind is clear. I've found my fitness passion; I never would have been on two wheels if I hadn't made The Speech. And, of course, it's what led me to my first reinvention.

Money

I sometimes think about a story I once heard about a billionaire who bought a Monet painting and didn't even hang it up – it stayed in its bubble wrap, leaned against the wall. It's sad to have so much money that spending it doesn't give you any pleasure. When I used to spend money, I rarely got any lasting pleasure out of it. When you're rich, it feels like the money pot is bottomless.

The upside of losing it all was that I learned to appreciate the things I buy so much more. When I spend money now, I get a lot of pleasure out of it. I only spend money on the things I need and really want, like my new carbon fibre bike. I love it, I use it every day, and I get real pleasure from it.

People think that if you become a millionaire, you're a million times happier than somebody who's not. Life isn't like that. There are plenty of upsides to being a millionaire, but it's not a direct ticket to happiness.

Speeches

If I hadn't made that terrible mistake, I wouldn't be doing any speeches (or, at least, no good ones). The whole core of the speech I give today is The Speech that led to my downfall. I do a speech about speech. If it wasn't for my downfall and my reinventions, nobody would be interested in my story, and I wouldn't have made a career as a public speaker.

I love giving speeches; it makes such a difference when you get pleasure from what you're doing. My pain led to that pleasure.

Advice to my younger self

I think about the Gerald Ratner from 1991. I think about who he was and what I would have advised him as a mentor. Here's what I would have said:

Wallowing in your own grief is the worst thing you can do, and blaming everybody else is not going to get you anywhere. It's not a question of how much money you earn. It's a question of using your brain and doing something, however lowly it might seem right now. This is a game of snakes and ladders: you've gone down a snake, and it doesn't feel good. But you can't give up, you just have to start looking for a ladder. You have to find the courage to get out there; the biggest mistake you can make is to not take the risk.

Rob: everything is a paradox

What really strikes me about Gerald's story is that his blunder, his downfall and his comeback gave him a different perspective on the life he so treasured. With the gift of hindsight, he could see that there were downsides to his glitzy lifestyle. That all the money in the world wasn't going to make up for the stress and the distance from his family.

Nothing is ever only good. And equally, nothing is ever only bad. What is good shall pass. What is bad shall pass. There is upside in all apparent downside, and downside in all apparent upside.

When you have a challenge or disruption, or something that you perceive to be all downside, there's actually upside in it. You know that logically, but emotionally, when you're feeling down, depressed, lost, it's very hard to see the upside. Or you simply don't want to, like when someone tells you that 'it'll be ok', or 'you'll learn a lot from it', when you just want to tell them to f*** right off. And sorry to rain on your parade, but there are always hidden downsides too. Not wrong-sides, there's nothing wrong in downsides, they're just there as part of the balance equation. Like equal support and challenge. Too much of either extreme and you lose balance and go into chaos.

In reality, I believe all situations have an equally balanced upside and downside. It's easy for you to look at someone else's life and see the upside in their despair and the downside of their success. But the wisdom is in being able to look at your own life and situations and challenges and say 'ok, I feel high, what are the potential downsides, so I don't get too ahead of myself?' Or 'I feel down now, but what are the potential upsides I can see that can lift me back into balance?' Wisdom is in seeing the balance at the time, not long after the event when it is always clear.

So if you get made redundant, what's the upside? Well, maybe you're forced to take some time off. Maybe you're forced to re-evaluate your life – something you should have done 20 years ago. Maybe you're forced to manage your finances better. Maybe you realise that comfort wasn't actually that good for you, giving you the bump you need to make a change. I've been fired three times, twice by my dad. And each time, it was a massive blessing in disguise.

Think about the worst thing that's happened to you this month. What is the upside? Here are some ideas:

You lose your job	⇨	you get more time with your family
You crash your car	⇨	you get fit by cycling everywhere
Your partner leaves	⇨	you can finally get a cat (they were allergic)
Your business fails	⇨	you get the spark of starting something new
You lose your money	⇨	you get good and budgeting and appreciate spending
You're attacked by critics	⇨	you take the useful feedback and grow

If you're in the depths of depression, it's going to be really hard to see the upside. Mental health is important, and it's something we all need to take seriously. That might mean talking to someone, reaching out for help. There is an upside, a way out, and you'll find it if you get support. There are helplines, doctors and therapists, and treatment you can take. Don't do it alone.

And if you don't feel you need a professional, but you do want to talk, please reach out to me – I'd be happy to help you. My email is rob@ robmoore.com, and I have talked to, supported and helped thousands of people one-to-one. If I can, I will try.

Focus on the upside

You get more of what you focus on. What you appreciate, appreciates. That's the idea behind goal setting, visualisation, targets and plans. If you imagine yourself doing something, achieving something, getting something, going somewhere, being someone, you're more likely to adjust your behaviour to make that happen. Especially if you add feeling and emotion to it, too.

When you're reinventing yourself, a big part of whether you succeed will be whether you believe you will succeed. We all have weaknesses, but there's a paradox here too: your great strengths are the yin to the yang.

Your strengths and weaknesses are intrinsically linked and cannot be separated. Impatience is good for progress and bad for progress. Thinking big will grow you big but you will miss out the details. Being deluded means you can achieve things at a scale that others don't believe possible. All strengths are weaknesses and weaknesses are strengths, at the extremes. Rather than focusing on your weaknesses, you need to focus on your strengths. Build them, rely on them.

Your emotions will probably get in the way of this, at least at first. Sadness, fear and anger will pull you down, cloud your head and hold you back. Part of success in business comes from managing your emotions: emotional mastery is business mastery. Control your flip-outs, smile at the people who piss you off, bite your tongue. Stop making assumptions – see reality for what it is.

Psychologist Prof. Lisa Feldman Barrett says that, as 'architects of our experiences', we can control our emotions – they don't control us. In her book *How Emotions Are Made: The Secret Life of the Brain*, she shares different ways to help you master your emotions. Here's my take on a few of them:

Healthy body

Eat well, exercise, sleep enough. Research has shown that keeping your body healthy and in motion helps you maintain a healthy emotional life. So make sure your schedule includes the gym and an early night.

Emotional intelligence

Emotional intelligence is the ability to identify and manage emotions – yours and other people's. It's about learning the right words to accurately describe how you're feeling – just 'good' and 'bad' leaves things fuzzy. The better you can describe how you're feeling, the better you can respond.

Life experience

Get out there, meet new people, go to new places, do new things. The more you're exposed to the world, the more able you'll be to deal with problems. (It will also give you the chance to spot opportunities.)

Awe

Make time to experience things that make you say 'WOW' – stunning sunrises, walks in nature, documentaries about amazing things. And remember to remember your positive experiences: keep a diary, or a happy jar, or just a vault in your memory, where you can go to and relive the good stuff.

By focusing on the upside, you'll have a much better chance of getting back in the game and reinventing yourself.

There's always a lesson – you just have to learn it

There is a gift in everything, and often it's a lesson: your disaster can be a powerful learning moment. And that lesson is something nobody can take away from you.

Look at the Coronavirus pandemic. Early on in lockdown, I interviewed Grant Cardone for my Disruptive Entrepreneur podcast. He was in the middle of a social media storm – he had made a joke video that didn't land well, and there was a big backlash. (He should have read Gerald's book and learned from his mistake!)

We were talking about the pandemic, and of course, it hit his business just like everyone else's. Here's what he said to me:

'What I've learned from this is you always need to be waiting. You need to have a bit of a sceptical eye, but not see everything as a scam. Because there's a big difference. I know this virus will pass, and on the other side of it, people are going to be better, people are going to be bigger, or they're going to be worse, and they're going to be smaller. It's up to the individual. Everybody can turn this into an opportunity if they elect to… the people that say "hey, I'm shifting right now, I'm going to pivot right now, I'm going to use all this energy and shift into the next stage of my life and mature and really become somebody" are going to be the superstars.'

One of the biggest words of 2020 was 'pivot' – businesses suddenly had to get agile and make fast, effective changes. People changed careers, moved house or country, turned classroom education into online learning, started new ventures.

While it was undoubtedly traumatic, it also called on people to think about who they are and what they want. What their business model is about. What direction their lives were going in. What their values were. Who they wanted to spend time with. Never before have we been blessed with such an opportunity to reflect on our lives.

When disruption is forced on you, I believe you have a great opportunity to turn it into a win. Whatever has led you to this point, this is your chance to reinvent yourself. The world is waiting to meet the new you. Get on with it! And remember this: if you don't risk anything, you risk everything.

Your Reinvention Toolkit

We have shared many exercises and approaches in this book. Here they are in one place, as an easy reference.

What is pushing your reinvention?

1. Write a list of the external and internal forces acting on you.

2. For the first item on your list, write down how it's affecting you. Is it a positive or negative impact? Is it real or imagined? Which direction is it pushing you in?

3. Now write down three ways it could be pushing you to reinvent yourself. Make one of them quite small and simple, something you could imagine yourself doing, and make one of them outrageous. The idea here is to shake up your thinking a bit. Don't worry if they're not focused, you just want to get your imagination working.

4. Repeat this for all the things on your list.

5. Circle or underline recurring themes. Is there anything that surprises or excites you?

Reset your internal monologue

1. Notice when you're making an excuse. Literally stop yourself and say 'that's an excuse' – say it out loud (don't worry about the weird looks you'll get). The more you call it out, the more conscious you'll be of it and the less power it will have. This is called a pattern interrupt: you want to break your internal dialogue habits and change what you say to yourself.

2. Write a new script. What would help you more than those harmful excuses? Give yourself some power with three positive messages. Here are some examples: 'I can do anything I want!' 'I love [singing, property investing, writing, or whatever your passion is] and I will do it.' 'I am strong.' 'I am confident.' 'I am enough.' These affirmations are short,

powerful statements you say to yourself (the mirror is optional). This is called a reframe. To turn the negative self-talk into a positive message. 'I can't' turns to 'How can I?'

3. Every time you catch yourself in one of your excuses (or any other negative self-talk, actually), choose one of your three affirmations and say it to yourself. Out loud, if you can. Say it over and over.

How to embrace change

1. Accept the inevitability of change. I'm constantly changing, constantly in the process of reinvention. Anybody who thinks that they can just sit back and repeat the same thing and the business or the success will come to them is wrong. Accept that change is constant and will happen. (If you find change traumatic, there's a whole process to get to the acceptance part, but for now, let's leave it at the goal.)

2. Observe reality. Once you've accepted that change is inevitable, it's easier for you to see reality the way it is, because you will recognise that you may have a filter of expectation over things. Keep your eyes open and try to spot things as they start to shift. That way, you'll be able to spot change on its way.

3. Make the connection. With a view of what's changing and what may be to come, you can start to make connections: what does the change mean for you? What impact will it have on your life and your business? How can you pivot to be successful in the new situation?

4. Take action. JFDI, as Rob says. It's easier said than done, of course, but sometimes you have to jump in (see chapter 6). The key thing to remember is whatever decision you're making, it is highly unlikely to be a rest-of-your-life decision. You don't write the whole book in one go, you do it chapter by chapter. You are taking action for this chapter, this scene, maybe just this sentence. Very few things can't be undone.

5. Repeat. Every day. Over and over. The more you do it, the more you'll get used to it and embrace it in your life.

How could you reinvent yourself?

For each of these areas of your life, think about one or more ways you could reinvent yourself. Write them down.

- Work – your business or your job

- Finance – your assets and cash

- Romantic relationship – your significant other (or others... I'm not here to judge)

- Friendship – the people you choose to spend time with

- Family – the people you're most closely connected to

- Home – where you live

- Body – your physical self

- Mind – your knowledge and mental capacity

- Spirit – your spiritual self, your essence and values

Choose up to three and dive deeper into the possibilities – create a vision board or write a letter from your future self.

Fear setting

1. Define, prevent, repair. Make three columns on a page. In column one, write down all the worst things that could happen if you do the thing you fear. In column two, write down all the ways you could prevent those things from happening. In column three, write down how you could fix things or who you might ask for help if the worst happened.

2. Look for the benefits. What would be the upside of trying, or moving towards your goal, even if you don't make it all the way? Make sure you include lessons you'll learn from the process.

3. Consider the cost of inaction. Doing the thing is scary, because you fear failure. But what would happen if you didn't even try? If nothing changed? If you didn't take action? Write it down. Thinking about the potential pain of the status quo can help you overcome your fears of taking the step and putting yourself at risk of failing.

Overcoming fear

- **(Re)define failure.** What would real failure look like compared to what you're worried about? What you're worrying about isn't that bad compared to the worst that could happen, so reset the bar – think about what failure actually is.

- **Feel the fear.** Don't try to dampen it or hide it or ignore it, really sit with it. Letting yourself fear it will show you it's not as bad as you might expect. Face reality. See things for how they are. Swallow, cringe, look at your failure head on.

- **Visualise obstacles.** When you look at your obstacle, you can also see it as a challenge – one you want to overcome. Like a mountain you're excited to climb, a race you want to try and win. Make your obstacle clear, and you're more likely to overcome it.

- **Reframe your goals.** Maximise the upside of failure before it (potentially) happens by setting learning goals. What can you learn from the thing you want to do, even if you fail? There's always a lesson to be learned; if you make it a goal, you will never fail.

- **Learn from other people's failures.** The more you're exposed to failure, even if it's someone else's, the more you'll put out your fear fire. It will become normal, less scary and you'll start to see failure as something you can handle.

- **Be kind to yourself.** This is something we forget, I think. The world is harsh enough as it is; be compassionate with yourself. Forgive yourself. Let yourself learn and carry on with your life, don't let those critical voices tell you to quit.

What's the smell in your room?

Take these steps to breaking your bad habits.

1. **The big stuff.** What in your life do you know you need to change? Think about the bigger picture here, the significant stuff. Family, relationships, career, finance, home, mind, body, soul. Write a list and stay objective – look at this as an outsider.

2. **The little stuff**. Now look at each of the items on your list in turn. What smaller, less visible habits are contributing to the rut? Try to spot patterns and habits that may not be working for you.

3. You should now have a list of habits that are not serving you – habits that are making your room smell. Habits contributing to more than one rut could be your best priorities for change. Rank your habits from 1 to 3 in terms of priority.

4. Start changing your bad habits!

Visualise your SMART goals

Set a goal related to your reinvention – make it:

- Specific

- Measurable

- Achievable

- Realistic

- Time-bound

Imagine you've achieved your goal. Read this, then close your eyes and go through the steps:

1. Where are you? What is around you? What does it look like?

2. Who are you with? What is it like to be with them?

3. How do you feel emotionally – are you happy? Satisfied? Relieved? Excited?

4. Now engage your other senses: how does it feel, physically? How does it smell, taste, sound?

Exercise your brain

Things you can do right now to keep your brain healthy:

*   Learn a new language.

*   If you want to watch TV, choose something you can learn from, like a documentary.

*   Listen to podcasts that will make you think.

*   Listen to audiobooks that will inspire you.

*   Read books – fiction, non-fiction, self-development – open your eyes, get your mind thinking.

*   Play a challenging game.

Eight ways to take care of your mental health

1. Don't compare yourself to others. We tend to descend into comparison when we're feeling low, so we end up comparing our lowest selves to other people's highest selves. If you notice you're doing it, stop yourself and say, out loud if you can, 'there's no comparison.'

2. Remember you're doing well enough… If you notice you're being harsh on yourself, take a minute to sit down and write a list of the things you have achieved, the things you can be proud of, to remind yourself you've got this.

3. … And you're good enough. Everyone has a purpose on this planet. You are valuable. You matter to people. We weren't all born geniuses or prodigies or maestros. I like to say every master was once a disaster – we all grew to where we are today.

4. Ask for help. If you feel alone, under-appreciated, unrecognised or misunderstood – or all of them – you need to ask for help. Mentors, advisors, therapists – there are people beyond your own family, friends and colleagues who can support you.

5. Master your schedule to deal with the pressure of daily life. The basic steps are: set the priorities in your life and work; block time in your calendar for these important things first; schedule everything else around this.

6. Be yourself, forget the judgement. If you go out there warts and all, you'll see that what you get back in terms of support and love and connection is so much more meaningful, as it's aligned with the real you.

7. Turn the trolls around. Trolls and critics and haters, keyboard warriors, bullies. When you fight hate with hate, all you do is make the hate grow. Try a bit of love – you'll both feel better for it.

8. Read Rob's book *I'm Worth More*. This book is full of strategies to promote mental health, and it could be a great support on your reinvention journey.

Start without scaring yourself rigid

1. Start while someone else is paying your bills. There's no harm in starting to explore your idea with the security of a monthly salary, especially if you're nervous about taking a leap.

2. Study the competition. You don't need to hire in a market research company and carry out expensive surveys with enticing incentives to get the lay of the land, but you'd be foolish not to study the competition. It costs nothing to do that.

3. Sell your product before you buy it. My acid test is this: sell the thing, see if people will pay for it. Do this and you can still walk away with no risk whatsoever, but with a very good idea of how the market will respond.

4. Go it alone, for a while at least. Don't jump the gun, rent big offices and hire staff; slow down and enjoy the ride. Part of the fun of starting out is doing everything yourself.

Start now, get perfect later

1. Start. Suck it up and get going. Just fuckin' do it.

2. Set a goal for your first milestone. Now you've got a bit of momentum, think about your minimum viable product (MVP) – what could you put out into the world that's on your path to your goal? Think beta versions, prototypes, mood boards.

3. Set KPIs. These could be anything but should be relevant to what you're trying to achieve.

4. Review. When you reach your first milestone, review where you are.

5. Tweak. Adjust what you're doing based on step 3. This is important: do it without judgement. This is the beauty of the testing approach – you just keep adjusting until you reach the sweet spot.

6. Repeat. Set more milestones with KPIs. Take more steps. Adjust what you're doing. Rinse and repeat.

7. Scale. Scale big and scale with lower risk; scaling too slow or too fast is dangerous.

8. Know when to quit. Quitting isn't necessarily a bad thing. Recognise when it's time to walk away.

7 steps to making risk more palatable

1. 'What if' is a useful thought; it stops you being reckless (just don't let it rule you). Don't deny your 'what ifs', just manage them.

2. What if it *does* work? It's wise to maintain balance and perspective. If you're asking yourself 'what if it doesn't work?' then you should ask yourself 'but what if it *does* work?' Look at the worst case, likely case and best case.

3. There's only one way to know: try. *Test*. See your journey not as an all-or-nothing, black-or-white equation, but as a continual test or series of very small tests and tweaks. If what you do works, repeat. If it fails, tweak. Then repeat.

4.   Create a plan. Chunk it down. Set your goal in the future, work back to today, break down the steps and metrics required to get there, and do them daily.

5.   Get a coach or mentor. Who is the easiest person to lie to? You've got it: yourself. Find a coach or mentor who's been there and done it. It's the shortest route to the most lasting success.

6.   Create accountability. You could put your goals out on social media and tell everyone you know, set up competitions with friends, competitors or even foes, pay or pledge money to charities. Try different approaches.

7.   Ninety-nine percent of the things you worry about never happen, so… GOYA and JFDI.

How to do the unpopular thing

1.   Look in the opposite direction. Notice where everyone else is going and explore what the opposite of that is.

2.   Think. Purposefully spend 15 minutes a day (at least) really thinking about an aspect of your reinvention, with no distractions. Take notes and you'll see where this takes you.

3.   Be sceptical. Stop trying to feel better by believing everything and instead, question everything. You'll soon start to see a more realistic picture of the world, and that will open up opportunities for you.

Designing your routine

(Read Rob's section in chapter 8 for the rocks-pebbles-sand analogy)

1.   Name your rocks. What is most important to you? What could you absolutely not live without? Think about family, health, maybe a hobby that makes your heart sing, walks with your dog, your reinvention. These are KLAs (Key Life Areas) and KRAs (Key Result Areas).

2.   Identify your pebbles. You might find things like your career, friends, business and house here. These include IGTs (Income Generating Tasks).

3. Identify your sand. What are the other things in your life, the little things you could do without but always seem to end up getting ticked off first? This includes doing things that are on other people's lists.

4. Get a year's worth of clear weekly calendar pages – you're going to start from scratch. Choose whatever format works best for you.

5. Add things in this order: rocks, pebbles, sand. Block out time for each thing; within each block, you can then set out the tasks you're going to complete when you get to it.

Build your support system

These are the people who will support your reinvention – make sure you have them all in your life, and nurture your relationships.

Family and friends: The people who are closest to you in your life, they are the ones who will love you no matter what happens. They're your cheerleaders, your unconditional supporters.

Peers: your colleagues; people you can talk to about your daily issues, who you can ask for advice and bounce ideas around with.

Heroes: The people you aspire to be like. You might connect with them through books (I read a lot of autobiographies) and other content.

Coaches: People who hold your hand and ask you questions to help you make good decisions.

Mentors: People who have been in your position, who's one or more steps ahead of you and who can help guide you in the right direction.

The basement: Your critics, haters and trolls – take the useful feedback, kill them with kindness or block them.

Learn active listening

1. Pay attention to what people say. Block out all distractions – put your phone away. Actively process their words as you hear them.

2. Make sure you understand them. Summarise what they've said or repeat words or phrases back to them. Even better: ask open ended questions if there are things you want to clarify or explore.

3. Respond, but don't interrupt. Listen, clarify, then pause before you speak. You'll find it makes for a much more interesting conversation for you both.

Build your own education system

Here are the elements to include in your Real Life University education.

Mindset development

Curiosity is the key: wanting to learn from everyone, wanting to learn everywhere you go, being fascinated about the world around you and always seeing new opportunities. Cultivate a sort of wonderment about people in the world. That is the greatest open mindset for learning and development, and that's what will fuel your reinvention, whatever area of your life it's in.

Knowledge acquisition

If you know what knowledge gaps you need to close, you can figure out how to patch them up fast, with books, podcasts, documentaries, online courses and professional training, for example. Another way to acquire knowledge is to travel – get out of your home and go exploring; learn about other professions, other markets, other hobbies.

Skill development

When you've mastered (or even just got a bit familiar with) digital tools, you've got endless opportunities to learn and be successful online.

Learning from people

Learn from people you like and people you admire, but also the people you (think you) dislike or disagree with. Being open minded to learn from people you don't like, or people have different beliefs, is really powerful.

Disrupt yourself

Disrupting yourself means challenging your thinking, challenging your strategies, looking at how you need to protect yourself from downside risk. This exercise will get you started:

1. Imagine you are your competitor. How would you try and take you out?

2. What flaws would you pick on if you were attacking you?

3. You're you again. How could you disrupt yourself now to pre-empt the strike?

Be ready for disruption

1. Write flexibility into your plan. Having a rigid plan in place for your reinvention might help you implement it, but it could slip you up if you need to adjust. Think about how you can inject some flexibility into your plan, to allow for changes.

2. Be inquisitive. We've seen why it's important to listen actively and be curious; apply that to disruption and you'll be better able to spot risks and opportunities that could force changes. Keep asking questions. Stay humble.

3. Keep your eyes open. Like Gerald says, be Columbo.

4. Work on your confidence. Believe in your ability to reach your goal, no matter what shifts and obstacles you come across.

Master your emotions

Healthy body: Eat well, exercise, sleep enough.

Emotional intelligence: learn the right words to accurately describe how you're feeling. The better you can describe how you're feeling, the better you can respond.

Life experience: Get out there, meet new people, go to new places, do new things. The more you're exposed to the world, the more able you'll be to deal with problems.

Awe: Make time to experience things that make you say 'WOW'. Keep a diary, or a happy jar, or just a vault in your memory, where you can go to and relive the good stuff.

References

We've mentioned people and resources throughout this book; here are some references you might want to take a look at, in order of appearance in the book.

Chapter 1

- One of the countless Countdown episodes Gerald watched: https://www.youtube.com/watch?v=WZhJDfyYW_o&list=PLiwpQ6MdERWP XmJ2Tnw5-0-zgsPcrJd0Q&index=37

Chapter 3

- Tim Ferriss' Fear-Setting exercise: https://tim.blog/2017/05/15/fear-setting/

- Gerald's take on Michael Gove (and the quote on bad decisions): https://www.thesun.co.uk/news/9261613/gerald-ratner-michael-gove-cocaine-joke/

Repeated failures

- Vera Wang's story: https://www.littlethings.com/vera-wang-figure-skating/ p63, repeated failures

- *Fast Company* article about James Dyson: https://www.fastcompany.com/59549/failure-doesnt-suck p60 Repeated failures

Chapter 4

- *Atomic Habits* by James Clear: https://jamesclear.com/atomic-habits

Playing it safe

- *New York Times* article on Kodak: https://www.nytimes.com/2008/05/02/technology/02kodak.html p78 Playing it safe

Chapter 5

- Sarah Silverman's tweet to a critic: https://twitter.com/sarahksilverman/status/946555534768979969

Arnie: Mr Reinvention

- Arnold Schwarzenegger's class of 2020 commencement speech: https://www.instagram.com/tv/CATvbrFgn7x/

- Arnold Schwarzenegger's famous speech: https://www.youtube.com/watch?v=Px7bjMyPA30

Risk-taker Richard Branson

- *Screw It, Let's Do It* by Richard Branson: https://www.virgin.com/branson-family/books/richard-branson/screw-it-lets-do-it Risk-taker Richard Branson

Chapter 8

- A review of *Strategy: The Indirect Approach* by B. H. Liddell Hart: https://www.foreignaffairs.com/reviews/capsule-review/1955-01-01/strategy-indirect-approach

  Timpson

- Interview with Sir John Timpson in the *Independent:* https://www.independent.co.uk/news/business/analysis-and-features/john-timpson-all-the-great-retailers-know-their-customers-does-ms-a6697471.html Timpson p137

- About the Timpsons: https://www.timpson.co.uk/about/meet-the-timpsons

Mae Jemison

- Mae Jemison: http://jemisonfoundation.org/about/mae-jemison/ Mae Jemison p155

Chapter 10

- *Iacocca: An Autobiography* by Lee Iacocca: https://www.goodreads.com/book/show/486319.Iacocca

- Ramit Sethi: https://www.iwillteachyoutoberich.com/ ch10

Chapter 12

- Lucy Kellaway on the Paul Tsongas 'deathbed' quote: https://www.ft.com/content/c7493e56-5a67-11dd-bf96-000077b07658 ch12 p197

- *How Emotions Are Made: The Secret Life of the Brain* by Prof. Lisa Feldman Barrett: https://lisafeldmanbarrett.com/books/how-emotions-are-made/ ch12 p202